Detroit Rich Boys

Muscles

iUniverse, Inc.
Bloomington

iUniverse books may be ordered through booksellers or by contacting:

iUniverse
1663 Liberty Drive
Bloomington, IN 47403
www.iuniverse.com
1-800-Authors (1-800-288-4677)

ISBN: 978-1-4502-9645-8 (sc)
ISBN: 978-1-4502-9646-5 (ebook)

Library of Congress Control Number: 2011905451

Printed in the United States of America

iUniverse rev. date: 03/04/2011

This book is dedicated to my late father, who was a living example of hard work and determination; to my mother and sister, for never giving up on me; to my soon-to-be wife, for staying strong through the hard times; to the few friends and family members that believed in me; and to my beautiful daughter, who recent decision to go to college, became the best decision she could have ever made.

Preface

Although I wrote the first draft of this book in only eight months, it was really a lifetime in the making. What gave me the idea to write this story was the interest I received whenever I told my gang stories. It was a major challenge at first. I did not know how to write a book until I tackled this project. I am a forty-four-year-old, self-taught writer; I relied on my natural abilities to tell this story. However, when I was growing up, I was an avid reader. I read comic books and novels as a youth. I also was an "A" student throughout my school years when it came to essays and book reports. I tried to write a story when I was thirteen but never completed it, as the streets became my new world. I did not think about writing again until I was thirty-eight. Since then, I have written three unpublished books; with each one, I learned more and more about writing. I plan to publish more stories and establish myself as a writer of different kinds of stories.

I wrote this book to tell the story of violence and gang activity in Detroit's public schools. Recently, thirty-four schools in Detroit were closed down because of low attendance and low funding. That number was shocking to me, but what was even more shocking than that is how the Detroit school system, along with other businesses and institutions, are being ignored. I am a product of gang activity; I sold drugs, and I also used drugs as a youth, but I changed. If I can change, others could change, schools could change, the ghetto could change, and the way we look at Detroit could change.

In order for any of that to happen, we should not discourage kids by closing their schools or kicking them out of their schools. We need to find better solutions than alienating troubled youths from each other. We have to work with each other. Some people believe that we should kick out the kids who don't want to learn and only teach the ones who do. I don't believe this. I believe every kid, bad or good, should have the opportunity to learn and further his or her education.

Introduction

Detroit is the home of the auto industry and the birthplace of many famous singers, entertainers, boxers, and notable civil rights leaders. But Detroit is also a dangerous city. The kids in Detroit's inner city schools are subjected to violence almost every day. However, most of the Detroit public schools during the eighties (the time of this story) were fair and decent. There were many public high schools with high levels of academic achievement, including Renaissance, Cass, Benedictine, and Ford. You had to have a high grade average to attend them. Young gangsters who attended inner city schools called them nerd schools, and kids from those nerd schools called the inner city schools thug schools. The most volatile gangsters attended Central High, Highland Park, and Cooley. Those were probably the most violent schools on the west side of Detroit. But there was another school that had even more gangs and more violence: Mumford High.

Mumford's west side gangs included the Six Mile Lunatic Assassins (LAs), the Seven Mile Black Killers (BKs), the Eight Mile Sconies, the Fenkle Avenues (FAs), and the Puritan Avenues (PAs), and there were also a few members from the Pony Down and the 20/20 Gangs. Basically, every neighborhood in the city had a gang from their hood. The gangs in Detroit were not influenced by outsiders, unlike many southern cities, which had gangs influenced by outsiders from California and New York. Most thug schools were usually ruled by gangs from their districts. Mumford, though, had gangs from all over the west side.

During the turbulent eighties, drugs and gang warfare became stronger in the streets and in the schools. The story you are about to read is violent, but it is not meant to promote or glorify gang violence. Most of the names of the characters have been fictionalized, but they are based on real-life individuals. The events are accurate, except for a few situations that were deliberately altered to protect the privacy of the living and the deceased.

1

This story begins with me, James Mussellistine. Most of my friends couldn't pronounce my last name right, so I adopted the name my friends have been calling me since I was twelve: *Muscles*. I didn't look muscular at all, but the strength I possessed for my slim size very much fit my persona. I'm sixteen years old, a black kid living on a street off Six Mile Road but who grew up with kids from across Puritan Avenue. I'm in tenth grade, I graduated from Beaubian Junior High last year, and now I go to Mumford High. Beaubian is located in the heart of the Eight Mile neighborhoods. My cousin, Moe, talked me into enrolling in Beaubian so the two of us could hang out more. But my one year in Beaubian was far from a fun one. It was a mistake enrolling in a school totally out of the hood and dealing with all those funny-talking Eights. It was like they had their own way of talking. It's safe to say the Eight Mile kids had a different accent from the rest of Detroit. Thoughts of my Beaubian days faded away as I walked the Mumford halls, anxious to see my friends. They were supposed to meet me on the first floor before my first hour class began.

My wait was over as three of my friends from Puritan Avenue approached me excitedly. "What's up, dog?" said Niddy, a slim, handsome, but dangerous-looking teenager.

"About time you made it to this motherfucker; I was starting to wonder if your ass was going to show up."

"It's ten more of us," Z-ooh said, with a hard, grim look that showed he was ready for action. Z-ooh was easily one of the strongest and most intimidating PAs, and no disrespect to the kid, but he looked like a gorilla when he was mad.

Then there was Uddia, who was also excited to see me.

"It's time to show you where the PA's lockers are; follow me. Every gang in the school has their own hall of lockers, and ours is branching out this year," he said.

If anybody from the Puritan neighborhood was stronger than Z-ooh, it was Uddia. He led us all to the second floor with a walk that made anyone in his path move out of the way. He was big and could have been considered fat, but those who knew him knew better. He was a solid three hundred pounds and very quick for his size, but most of all, he never showed mercy in a fight. Uddia and Niddy were the leaders of the PAs in Mumford. When we reached the lockers, Jerry, an old friend of mine, ran up to me with glee in his eyes.

"What's up, Muscles? Where you been hiding at, dog? I haven't seen you in a minute," he said excitedly while exchanging daps.

While Jerry and I talked about old times, Z-ooh, Uddia, and Niddy stared angrily at the skinny kid who interrupted their tour of the lockers. If looks could kill, Jerry would be dead right now, but the three kept their thoughts to themselves and continued to stare Jerry down. I noticed the glares from the start and ended my conversation with Jerry.

"I'll catch up with you later, Jerry," I said. "I got some PA business to take care of."

Jerry looked confused about why I was brushing him off like that, but he understood fully when he saw my PA friends.

After Jerry left, Niddy resumed our conversation about the lockers. "This is your locker, Muscles. You got two sides in it, but it's best to use the other as an alias, you know, get a nerd to take one side, then you can hide your shit there—" Before Niddy could finish his sentence, Uddia cut him off.

"It's best to get a female because the cops and the tru's usually don't check bitches' lockers here."

"Right, we got about fifty lockers together, about twenty-five on both sides of the hall. And to think, just last year we only had twenty," Z-ooh added.

"Yeah, but those Sevens and Eights have the most lockers in the school. It's way more of them than us," Niddy retorted.

After Niddy's statement, Uddia and an Eight Mile Sconie named Frog made eye contact and stared each other down till they were almost out of each other's view. "PA down," Uddia chanted, just before Frog left his sight. His voice traveled through the halls, and other kids in the hallway stared at Uddia and then looked away when he noticed them. This was common with the squares and nerds who went to Mumford. If you weren't part of a gang, you stayed clear away from them, simple as that. The gangs in Mumford had their own chants as a sign of representation, no finger signs, no colors, just a cry out of your hood's name. However, different gangs did wear different styles of coats and jackets, but it was not because of the colors. Most of the kids in the city wore jackets from the local sports teams, but the bangers wore jackets from their favorite teams. The PAs wore Pirates and Phillies jackets, while the Eight Mile Sconies and the Eight Mile Smurfs wore Yankees jackets. The Six Mile Lunatic Assassins (LAs) wore Dodgers jackets, and the Seven Mile Black Killers (BKs) sported Royals jackets. After my friends and I hung our belongings in the lockers, we all went to class. Uddia, however, still had Frog on his mind, and none of his thoughts about him were good.

After school was over, I met twelve of my friends at the Dexter bus stop. Some members had left earlier, while others hung around the school trying to get acquainted with all the new girls from their classes. When the bus came, Niddy and I were the first to get on. We both led the others to the back of the bus and quickly sat down.

Niddy and I were tight. All the PAs on the bus were cool with each other and were down for whatever, but my friendship with Niddy went beyond gang obligations. We had the same goal: to graduate together, which drew our friendship closer. When the bus got near my house on Six Mile and Fairfield, I pulled the cord to get off.

"Holler at me tonight," Niddy said as I went out the back door of the bus. "The PAs is having a first day of school get-together party; it's going to be plenty of girls there, so you better be there."

"Okay," I said.

Niddy and I lived on the same street, except Niddy's block was across Puritan, and mine began on Six Mile Road. All the other PAs lived across or near Puritan Avenue, southward from my house. My house is located in the neighborhood where the Six Mile LAs resided, and even though I had known them since I was much younger, I never joined their gang. I rarely even spoke to any of them but respected them, because of the respect they gave me. Anyone who knew me knew all my close friends were from across Puritan Avenue, but what most people didn't know is that I was part of the first wave of PAs that was formed two years ago, and I dedicated my young life for this cause. Uddia, Niddy, Roni, Z-ooh, Robin, Ant-Nice, Big-Tone, Boone,

Travis, Sugarman, Moon, Greg, Ant from Lawton, Perpin-Norm, and Sid-Money were the core of that first wave.

There's a thin line between the middle class Six Mile neighborhoods and the low-income Puritan neighborhoods. In fact, only three blocks separated Six Mile and Puritan.

There were other gangs across Puritan before the PAs, like the Puritan Players, the Moneymakers, and the Pretty City Flynn Boys. But none of those gangs lasted long. Before I made it to my steps, my mind wandered back to when I first met Niddy. I met him through Roni. Roni, who lived on the same street but on a different block, was Niddy's first cousin. He also was my closest friend. Their family was the largest in the neighborhood, with relatives on both sides of Puritan. My friendship with Roni led to my involvement with other PA kids, and eventually I was considered part of Roni's family and a member of the group.

Unlike Niddy and me, Roni didn't attend Mumford. He was two years younger than us and attended Hampton Junior High, a haven school in the Seven Mile area. The problems I had with the Eights in Beaubian were the same problems Roni was dealing with in Hampton with the Sevens. But like all PAs, he was well respected. That respect wasn't because of the gang's popularity, because we were barely known at this point. It was because of their individual reputations. Almost every kid from Puritan could fight, and we were known to fight even when outnumbered.

All low-income neighborhoods produced gangsters, hustlers, thieves, pimps, and whores. But in Detroit, the middle class and even some rich areas produced them too. On the west side of Detroit, the Six, Seven, and Eight Mile Gangs all lived in middle class neighborhoods. This was why poverty-ridden neighborhood gangs like the PAs, the FAs, and the Linwood Boys called the kids from the mile gangs "Rich Boys." The Rich Boy Gangs didn't get along with the ghetto gangs, simply because of their different lifestyles. The PAs and other ghetto gangs thought Rich Boys were spoiled brats, and Rich Boys thought ghetto youngsters were so broke and so gutter that they would do anything for money. I knew this fact probably more than anyone. I was considered a Rich Boy, but I hated it when anyone called me that. Being a Rich Boy and part of a gang from the ghetto gave me insight into political problems nobody else really cared about. I spent many nights across Puritan and knew that the living conditions over there were gravely different from mine.

Each mile gang had at least three hundred members on the street; some of the gangs began back in the sixties. For years Mumford was ruled by the Eight Mile Sconie Gang, and their war with the Seven Mile BKs was well known in the streets and in the schools. But a new generation of Eights called the Smurfs was taking the place of the Sconies who graduated or were kicked out. They were mostly freshmen and tenth graders who had graduated from Beaubian. Even the tenth-grade Smurfs were new to Mumford, because just like me they all graduated from Beaubian after the ninth grade.

When I entered my house, the familiar smell of hot chili filled my nose. The long day in school plus the bus ride had taken a toll on my stomach, and getting to my mother's chili in the kitchen became a definite must.

"Hi you doing, Mom," I said, looking in the well-stocked refrigerator.

"I'll feel better when you wash your hands, boy! I tell you every day to wash your hands before you come in the kitchen; when you going to understand?"

"Sorry, Mom, it won't happen again."

Unlike most families across Puritan, I had two parents in my household. It was a luxury most of my friends didn't have; they had only one parent, while nearly all the kids on my side of Puritan had two. But the biggest difference between the two neighborhoods was the size of the houses and the security. My house, like all the others on my block, was a large brick house with an upstairs, an attic, and a basement, and it was protected by the police and a neighborhood security force. Most of the poverty-ridden houses across Puritan were only one level, and no security patrolled their streets. The double standard in these neighborhoods was very disturbing to me.

I ate my chili and went to my room with thoughts of staying home instead of going to the party. I knew I had to get up in the morning and go to school and felt it wouldn't be wise staying up late at a party. I put a kung fu movie in my videocassette recorder, turned it on, and flopped on the bed with sleepy eyes, which eventually closed.

After I woke up, I got out of bed and turned the TV off. When I looked at the clock, I was surprised that it was almost eight o'clock; I had been out for hours. I realized it was still early, so I decided to head over to the party.

Hell, I could hang out all night; I don't need any rest now, I thought as I got ready for the party.

2

On the second day of school, kids rushed anxiously through Mumford's entrance doors, where they were checked by truant officers and two Detroit policemen, Officers Steve Brooks and Ted Jones.

The Mumford Seven Mile leaders were Black Mike, Romeo, Hash, and P-Coal. They were all from a different Seven Mile neighborhood. Their rivalry with the Eight Mile Sconies had last more than ten years, and it intensified every year. There were about a hundred Seven Mile members attending Mumford. In previous years, the Eight Mile Sconies outnumbered the Sevens by staggering odds and dominated any gang that came against them.

Black Mike, who was very slim with a lot of heart, hated the Eight Mile Sconies with a passion. He beefed with them almost all of his young life and caught the bad end of the beefs last year, when he was a sophomore. The Eights bum-rushed him three times; the physical scars healed after a while, but his emotional scars never healed. He wanted revenge and wouldn't be satisfied until he got it. Given the chance, he would kill a Sconie or a Smurf, and anyone who was affiliated with them.

Last year, the Sevens and the Eights were in a lot of altercations, and because of the small number of Sconies attending Mumford this year, the Sevens came to school with confidence and a swagger. "This the year Seven Mile takes Mumford," Black Mike said, as he watched Officer Brooks search his friend P-Coal.

Officer Brooks and Officer Jones were two take-no-shit city cops who tried to keep order in Mumford. They would check the IDs of kids they thought were delinquent or search them for weapons and drugs. Officers Jones pulled Black Mike to the side and checked him for weapons. "You better concentrate on your schoolwork, stupid," he said. The Seven Mile leader glared at Officer Jones after the search and then proceeded to his first hour class, French.

There were nine Seven Mile members in Black Mike's French class, including Hash, the other Seven Mile leader. Me, Niddy, and Sid-Money were also in that class. Half the class was part of a gang, and the Seven Mile Gang was the deepest. Black Mike came into the classroom and walked to the back of the class; he told one of his boys to get up so he could have his chair. The Seven Mile kid gave up the chair like he was seating a king. Even the teacher, Mrs. Jackson, noticed Black Mike's smooth authority. He was the most popular Seven Mile member, mainly because of his battles with Eight Mile Sconies. Like the Eights, his group was very organized and always ready to strike in large multitudes. When one fought, they all fought.

Niddy and I were sitting in the middle row talking about last night's party, when a Seven Mile kid named Lee walked by and purposely stepped on my brand-new tens. Lee had never liked me. I had run-ins with him in elementary school, and since he joined the Sevens, it became apparent he wanted revenge.

After the disrespect, I wiped my shoe off, got out my chair, and stormed to Lee's table with both my fists clenched. "What you doin', bitch?" I yelled.

"Sit down, James!" Mrs. Jackson yelled. "Sit down now!"

Just as she said that, four Seven Mile members stood up with their fists balled. Niddy and Sid-Money responded by getting up out of their chairs, ready to fight. The violence seemed unavoidable as four more Sevens stood up. Unfortunately, the only Seven who didn't rise from his chair was the one I was towering over. Black Mike caught Lee's eyes and glared at him. Lee was Black Mike's cousin, but what Black Mike hated more than anything was a pussy, even if you were related to him.

"All right, people, have a seat or everyone that's standing up will be suspended," the heavy-set teacher said with emotion.

She knew she had to act immediately, or the standoff would escalate into an altercation. As she moved closer to Lee and me, the look on Black Mike's face suggested the next step his gang makes will have to be wise. He had bigger plans for Mumford than an easily won fight against a little-known gang like the PAs. He knew the PAs were fighters, but he must have felt that we were not organized enough to fuck with his group. "Everybody squat," Black Mike ordered, as he immediately sat down in his chair.

After the command, all of the Sevens sat down in their chairs also. Niddy and Sid-Money followed suit and sat down. But I stood my ground, continuing to loom over Lee with my fists balled.

"PA down, bitch," I said and then mashed my index finger on Lee's forehead.

"I'm giving you one more chance to sit down, James, or you, and only you, are going to the office," Mrs. Jackson said with authority.

Just the thought of going to the office on the second day of school was too much for me to think about. So I returned to my chair. As the class started to settle down, Black Mike gave Niddy and Sid-Money a look that said, "I'll get you later," and they both responded with smiles that seemed to irritate him to the bone. After the staredowns, Niddy looked at me with admiration.

When the class returned to normal, Black Mike sat back and daydreamed about the plan he had put together to rush the Eights today. That was the bigger plan Black Mike envisioned, not fighting the PAs, which were barely known. He wanted to take out the big fish while their numbers were low. While Mrs. Jackson passed out the day's assignment, he reviewed the strategy of his plan: the Sevens would attack the Eights in their own hallway before they opened their lockers. This way, the Eights could not get any weapons out before they attacked. Black Mike and P-Coal were to meet up after sixth hour and lead this attack while Romeo, Hash, and the others waited in getaway cars outside the school.

After another firm warning to the class, Mrs. Jackson let the kids leave five minutes before the bell rang. Niddy and I made sure we were the first to leave the class and waited for Sid-Money to come out. Black Mike and his gang of Sevens stared hard at Niddy and me when they walked past us in the hallway. When Sid-Money finally came out, we anxiously walked to our lockers, but the tension disappeared when Uddia arrived on the scene.

"Hey Uddia," I said, "I just came close, and I mean close, to whipping someone's ass in French."

"Oh yeah, what happened?" he asked.

Before I could reply, Niddy cut in and said, "We got into it with them Sevens in French, Uddia. One of them fools disrespected Muscles and was about to get handled—"

Sid-Money rudely interrupted, "I don't think so, Niddy; we were outnumbered something like ten to three. There was no way we were going to win that one."

Niddy and I looked at each other and smiled, and then we broke into laughter. Sid-Money looked confused; he couldn't understand why we were laughing until I opened my bag and he looked inside. The sight of the baby Uzi in my bag caused Sid-Money's heart to skip a beat. I always carried a sports bag with me. Niddy and Uddia were the only two in the school who knew what I actually kept in my bag.

"That's some heavy shit, man, but I think you better put it in your locker, dog; you're not in Beaubian, you're in Mumford. You got two real cops peeping everything out here," Sid-Money warned me.

"Fuck that, dog," I said. "Those Sevens and Eights love to rush people, and I'm not going to be one of them."

"He's right," Z-ooh added. "I rather kill seven fools then let seven fools kill me." The rest of the PAs started to crowd around their lockers after leaving first hour.

"You must know how to read minds, Z-ooh," I said. "How did you know it was that many Sevens in the class?"

"This girl I know is in your French class, she told me about the whole thing a few minutes ago," he replied.

The gangs in the school usually gathered around the lockers. Whenever something happened in one class, everyone in the school knew about it before the next class. When the bell rang, we had five minutes to get to class. The PAs said their good-byes to each other like family, and then we all headed to class.

A September rain started to pour on the troubled school. It was fourth hour, and Bam-Bam, an Eight Mile leader, and his right-hand boy, Frog, entered the third-floor bathroom with authority. Each one of the three floors in Mumford had a boys' and a girls' bathroom on it; the third-floor bathroom was part of the Eights' territory. If you weren't part of the Eight Mile Gang, you did not use that bathroom.

Niddy and I had walked into the bathroom a few times but weren't harmed because we both had relatives from Eight Mile neighborhoods. However, after getting cold stares from the Eights who didn't know us, we did not return to that bathroom.

Bam-Bam and Frog were two of the most dangerous Sconies in Mumford. They were both hard-core bangers from their hoods, but like me they were part of an upper middle class family that lived in a pretty good neighborhood. They attracted trouble like a magnet, got into many fights, and were known for many shoot-outs in the streets.

Frog took out a bottle of wine, and he and Bam-Bam started drinking it as soon as they came in the bathroom. Everyone smoked and drank in the Mumford bathrooms. For some reason, Mumford security never patrolled the Eights' bathroom. Some thought it was because the bathroom was up on the third floor; others thought it was because of their high respect for Eight Mile kids.

"Man, I can't wait to start practicing for football, Bam-Bam," Frog said, and then took a big swallow from the bottle. Frog's real name was Todd, but his massive body and large head had earned him the nickname "Frog."

"Yeah, I bet you can't wait to hit a motherfucker on that football field, but stay focused and be ready to hit somebody on the real field. The buzz going around the school is the Sevens are deeper than us for the first time," Bam-Bam said with concern.

Bam-Bam sold drugs because he liked to, not because he had to. His father worked at Chrysler, and his mother was a college teacher. His parents wanted to send him to a private school, but he refused and chose Mumford. While Bam-Bam and Frog were drinking the wine down, more Eights came into the bathroom. Some of them were Sconies, but most of them were in the new Eight Mile Gang called the

Smurfs. Like the PAs, the Smurfs were new to Mumford, and nobody had any idea how many of them were in the school ... except for me.

I attended ninth grade with a lot of Smurfs, and I was probably the only one in the building who actually knew how many Smurfs were in Mumford. My cousin Moe, who was an Eight Mile Sconie himself, had introduced me to a lot of them and had told me who was who in the new gang. Unlike the Sconies, the Smurfs were very much into the styles on their clothing. The New York jackets they wore were noticed all over the school. Bam-Bam chuckled to himself at the flamboyance of the new wave of Eights in the bathroom. Two Smurf leaders, Clyde and Billy, went straight to Bam-Bam and Frog and greeted them with hugs and daps. Although the two Smurfs had been Eight Mile leaders in Beaubian Junior High, Bam-Bam was clearly the Eight Mile leader in Mumford. The two Smurfs were wearing sagging Levis and the infamous New York jackets. The bell soon rang, and everyone reported to class.

Bam-Bam and Frog entered their sixth hour class, government. Sixth hour is the last class of the day for most of the kids in the school; however, some students were assigned a late class during seventh hour. Bam-Bam and Frog both needed credit from the late class to graduate this year. Rumors suggested; the mother of Danny, another Sconie, worked in the school's scheduling department. She made sure Danny and eight of his senior friends were in four classes together. She wanted to see Danny and his friends graduate together. She had no idea that she had helped keep Eight Mile Gang members together. All the Eights in the class were hard-core bangers, but they had made plans over the summer to chill out this year so they could graduate in June.

Before Bam-Bam and Frog sat down, they teased two girls who wore glasses, calling them squares and nerds, kicking off laughter from the class. The two Eight Mile Gang members laughed all the way to the back of the class, where Danny and the rest of the Eights were sitting. Mr. Steel, the teacher, was glad they went to the back for more reasons than one. He felt he could reach the kids who wanted to learn better if the bad apples in the class sat in the back, but he also feared them.

When the students rushed out of the class, Bam-Bam smiled at Danny. Danny's intelligence mirrored his high connections in the school, and his mother's calculated class arrangements had put the Eights in power positions no gang in the school could match. The Eights also enjoyed having their last class next to their lockers. Because of this, they were always the first in the school to make it to their lockers after sixth hour.

When they arrived at their lockers, Frog looked down the long hall and was concerned by the very low number of Sconies in the hallway. The Eights' hallway was always deep with members, but this year only half of those lockers in the hall were occupied by Sconies.

As Frog and the senior Eights were about to open their lockers, Black Mike and twenty-six of his Seven Mile boys stormed the hallway like a police raid. Danny was the first to notice the fast-moving mass of danger coming toward them. "Bam-Bam, look out!" he yelled, but the warning was too late as Black Mike and his boys attacked the Eights like a pack of starving wolves.

This was the moment Black Mike had dreamed of; his first wild punch landed on Danny's face, breaking his nose in two places and causing him to fall to the floor, screaming in agony. "Seven up, seven up!" Black Mike chanted as he kicked Danny numerous times after he fell to the hard Mumford floor.

Bam-Bam and Frog reacted quickly to the attack; they stood back to back and threw haymakers at anybody who came near them. The formation enabled them to swing with confidence, since no one could come up behind them while they fought. Unfortunately, the rest of the Eights were getting stomped unmercifully by the Sevens. Pandemonium filled the hallways as "Seven-up!" echoed loudly through the school.

Black Mike's battle plan was cold and calculated. The Sevens had caught the Eight Mile seniors clearly by surprise. "Five more minutes and we're out," Black Mike said to P-Coal, as the two continued to kick Danny while he was down.

"We should leave now! The damage is done," P-Coal said; he thought it was going way too easy. He had expected more resistance from the Eights.

"Not yet! We're going to stick with the plan and fuck these fools up." Just as Black Mike said that, he heard a loud grunt.

"Man, you see that?" P-Coal said. "Bam-Bam and Frog are knocking people out! We can't let them fools get away with that; it's time to handle up!"

He and Black Mike started making their way toward Bam-Bam and Frog, who were fighting like wild dogs. But before Black Mike and P-Coal got a chance to swing on the two Eights, they heard a thunderous rumble from the rear, causing them both to stop in their tracks. When they turned around to see what was making the noise, their jaws fell to the floor. At least fifty Eight Mile Smurfs were running down the hall. They quickly engulfed the Sevens and began chanting, "Eight o'clock!" as they struck the Sevens with short bats and pistols.

P-Coal was stunned, till a hard blow from a short wooden bat brought him back to the situation at hand. He started swinging, thinking that death could be the outcome, while Frog attacked Black Mike with a vicious clothesline, almost breaking his neck. Frog had noticed Black Mike and P-Coal coming toward him before the Smurfs had even joined the fight. So when Black Mike turned around to look at the Smurfs, Frog had made his move. The clothesline was something he would brag about for days to come.

Frog and Bam-Bam tended to their fallen homeys and then left the scene. Danny was the only Eight left; he couldn't leave after the beating he received. Even though he was in pain, a broken nose and a few bruises weren't going to stop him from getting revenge. He kicked Black Mike two times while he was down. The fast-acting Black Mike took out a pair of brass knuckles and popped up on his feet, looking to fight Frog, who had clotheslined him, but settling for Danny, who had kicked him. He swung his brass knuckles into Danny's midsection four times before the Eight fell to the floor once more.

Black Mike and his boys fought like warriors. But it was evident that the many Smurfs who came to the scene were wearing the Sevens down. P-Coal bit his lip in frustration as his boys fell right in front of him. All the kids around the melee quickly left the scene when the Smurfs pulled out their large pistols.

"Seven Mile pull out, Seven Mile pull out!" Black Mike yelled. Black Mike and P-Coal were holding they own, but they knew the tide had changed. They threw a few more punches and then motioned everyone to follow them out the door near the stairway. "Seven-up!" a few Sevens yelled while running through the exit doors. Only nine Seven Mile members made it out the exit. The others were at the mercy of the Smurfs. Black Mike hated to leave the fallen Sevens, but when he saw Officers Brooks and Jones coming down the hall, he knew they'd be all right.

As Black Mike and his group ran out of the school, the Smurfs were still on the third floor beating the shit out of the rest of the hapless Sevens. "Eight-o'clock, eight-o'clock," Clyde chanted as he cracked a Seven in the back with a bat.

The hallway was a bloody mess when Officers Jones and Brooks finally made it to the scene. "Stop, you idiots!" Brooks screamed, grabbing one of the gang members. The rest of the Eights ran at the sight of the officers. One of the truant officers called an ambulance, as the moans from the badly injured echoed through the hallway.

Black Mike led his boys through the crowd in the schoolyard. He gritted his teeth when he saw the last of the getaway cars turning the corner a few blocks away. "Shit," he said, "we gotta split up in threes since it's nine of us, and make it to the hood on foot." He realized the police would be looking for a gang of kids.

About ten minutes later, Black Mike, P-Coal, and White Boy ran into a store on Curtis Road.

"Man, I thought you said it wasn't that many Eights left in the school; we got our ass kicked back there," White Boy said.

"Quit crying and be happy you're one of the ones that made it out of the school," Black Mike said while he stopped to catch his breath.

The store was owned by Johnny, an older man who had taken over when his father died. Johnny was down with running numbers, and he ran drug safe houses in the past. But what Johnny was down with more than anything was Seven Mile. He had been a Seven Mile Gang banger when he was younger and always showed love to anyone from the Seven Mile neighborhood in his store. Black Mike was

Niddy lit up his joint, and I pulled one out of my back pocket, lit it up, and then passed it to Black Frost.

"Here, dog," I said, "let's get two flowing around this motherfucker."

Black Frost's gang, the FAs, were from Fenkle Avenue, about four blocks south of Puritan Avenue. Black Frost was well respected in Mumford and probably the most dangerous fighter in the school. Unfortunately, his gang only had nine members in the school, too few to do any gang fighting, which was why everyone in his gang sported guns on a daily basis.

"So, what you two think about the big fight last Friday?" he asked.

"You mean between the Eights and the Sevens?" I answered. "I saw the tail end of it, and it was definitely one to remember, Frost."

"Well, I seen the whole fight," Black Frost said. "Hell, I had to knock one of them out because I got too close to the action trying to see."

"Oh yeah, who did you knock out, a Seven or an Eight?"

"I couldn't tell; shit, if they don't wear they jackets, they all look like Rich Boys to me. I couldn't tell them apart."

"They don't need to wear their jackets for me to know who they are," Niddy said. "You're more familiar with gangs like the Rosa Park Boys and the Linwood Boys, gangs that are close to your hood, but these Rich Boy Gangs are different, Frost. They like to rush people, dog. Tell him, Muscles."

"Okay," I said. "I went to school with most of the Smurfs in junior high school, and even though my cousin is an Eight Mile member himself, I didn't trust them, and I sure in the fuck don't trust them now. The Sevens are very cocky too, they're also known to rush people, so be careful, Frost."

I took a long drag off the reefer and passed it to Niddy; when I looked at my watch, I noticed we only had two minutes left before the bell rang. Just then, Officers Jones and Brooks stormed through the bathroom doors with police clubs.

"All right, you idiots!" Officer Jones yelled. "Put the cigarettes and weed out, and go to class before I take everyone in here to jail."

Everyone ran out of the bathroom. Since Niddy and I were in the back of the bathroom, we were the last to leave, which caused us both to be late to our English class.

"You two are late again?" said Miss Johnson, the teacher. "In my class, attendance is 50 percent of your grade. So, if you pass all your assignments but flunk your attendance, you fail the whole course. Keep that in mind; now sit down and read today's assignment on the chalkboard." The fine, well-shaped teacher stood with her hands firmly on her hips.

Niddy and I both looked sheepishly at Miss Johnson before we took our seats in the back of the class. "Damn, dog, where you get that shit from?" Niddy whispered. My only response was the permanent smirk on my face that I always got when I was high.

My mind started drifting from the strong effects of the weed. I noticed Black Mike and Tim sitting in the front of the class. I wondered whether the feud between the Eights and the Sevens was going to escalate. But most of all, I wondered what effect it was going to have on the other gangs in the school. If gangs started choosing sides, the peace amongst other gangs would end. "Now that would be real fucked up," I said in a low tone, responding to my own thoughts.

Suddenly, I heard a familiar whistling sound coming from the hallway. It was the same melody from Saturday-morning cartoons. But it wasn't the melody that worried me; it was the whistlers: the Eight Mile Smurfs were the only ones who whistled that melody, and it usually meant some type of danger was about to happen. Only the Eights knew the whistling code, but since I had attended Beaubian, I also knew what it meant.

"Hey Niddy," I whispered, "we need to get the fuck out of here, dog; something is about to go down."

But before Niddy could respond, Billy, the Smurf leader, rushed into the classroom with his boys behind him. They stormed in and started attacking every Seven Mile member in the class. Pandemonium resulted, as all the kids jumped out of their seats to avoid the onslaught. The four Sevens were all caught off guard. Each one of them had a pair of brass knuckles in their pockets, but Black Mike and Tim were the only two to take them out in time. Their comrades, Keith and Curtis, gave all they had but were engulfed by the Eights. Billy's boys beat the two kids down in their chairs while the girls screamed in total fear. Miss Johnson screamed also and then ducked under her table to take shelter as chairs started to fly.

Black Mike and Tim swung their brass knuckles like their very lives depended on it, realizing there was no way out of the class except through the Smurfs, who blocked the path to the door. Other kids were trapped inside too, since the four Seven Mile members were sitting in the front of the class when the Smurfs attacked.

Black Mike and Tim fought the Smurfs aggressively, swinging their brass knuckles like wild animals. As the two continued to hold their own, Niddy and I were hemmed in the back, where most of the students had taken refuge. Billy and his boys started throwing more and more chairs as Black Mike and Tim moved out of the way. The many kids in the way helped their situation a great deal, although innocent students paid dearly for it. Four students had been knocked to the floor by flying chairs.

Tim gritted his teeth angrily when he noticed two Smurfs still beating on his unconscious friends. He ran at full speed and attacked them from behind with devastating blows. As he swung, he recalled all the Sevens who had gone to the hospital in last week's fight. His heroism, however, was for naught as six more Smurfs entered the classroom and joined the fray. The new Smurfs on the scene surrounded the two Sevens with chairs and broomsticks, but Black Mike kept four of them at bay with a chair of his own.

Meanwhile, Niddy and I were looking for a way out; the light from the hallway got dimmer as more Smurfs arrived and blocked the door.

"It's about to get messy," Niddy said, after realizing the window across the classroom was open. "Follow me!"

"Look, I see where you want to go," I replied. "I noticed that window too, but it's no different than the way to the door. Too many bangers and students are in the way; it's too dangerous."

"I got my dad's thirty-eight, and you got an Uzi in your bag, nigga; we're going across that room, and no Seven or Eight Mile nigga is going to stop us. Take your shit out, dog, and let's go," Niddy said as he whipped his gun out, held it high in the air, and started walking toward the window. I followed him with my hand on the Uzi in my bag, and even though I never took it out, my finger stayed glued to the trigger.

Niddy and I were halfway to the window when Tim was knocked down by several chairs. His screams made Black Mike's skin crawl, as he was forced to fight on or get knocked down too. Black Mike was so mad, he tore the flesh off someone's face with his next swing. But the Eight Mile bangers continued to beat Tim, kicking his battered body

respect gave him clout most members didn't have. Black Mike jumped in the tub with revenge on his mind.

Meanwhile, Niddy and I were just entering a store on Six Mile Road. We were thirsty from running so we bought a couple of pops, and we needed change to use the pay phone. We bought the pops and called Uddia's brother Joe to come pick us up. We waited outside the store for him to arrive; knowing the weapons we were carrying made us way too hot to keep footing it.

After waiting for fifteen minutes, Joe arrived in Uddia's car with an unhappy look on his face. He knew something major was wrong for us to beg him to pick us up. But he also knew he could get in trouble with Uddia for taking his car. Joe had been suspended from school, so he stayed at home and drove Uddia to school while he looked for a job. Now he feared his brother would be mad if he knew he had used the car.

"All right," Joe said, "before you tell me what happened, I want you both to promise me you won't tell Uddia I picked you up in his car."

"I promise," I said.

"I promise too."

"Good, now tell me what happened."

"We had to blast our way out of Mumford, dog," said Niddy, exaggerating the shooting incident.

"Yeah, those Sevens and Eights got in a beef today in class, and we had to bail up out of there," I added.

"Did anybody get smoked?"

"No," I said.

"Good."

Silence filled the air as Joe thought about attending Mumford. And even though the possibility was low because of his current situation, the thought came to mind every time he saw a PA from Mumford. He and his brother were so close, he felt he should be there too. Joe had knocked out many youngsters and hoped to become a professional boxer.

Joe turned down Puritan Avenue, and the fear Niddy and I had when we left Mumford was forgotten as we could see we were home free.

"We appreciate you picking us up like that, Joe; you were right on time with that shit," Niddy said. "We are most definitely going to pay you back for this, dog."

"Where are you two going?" he asked. "I would take you to my house and we all could get fucked up on this gold weed I got, but I don't want Uddia to even know I seen you guys."

"Drop us off at Boone's house. We'll chill out over there until school is out, and then we'll mob to the crib from there."

When Joe stopped, we got out of the car and thanked him again and started chanting our familiar battle cry, "PA down!" We continued chanting until we noticed Boone sitting on his porch. Boone responded by chanting the battle cry also. "PA down!" we chanted while exchanging daps on his porch. Boone, who was about three years older than Niddy and me, led us to his room in the basement.

"Where is your brother Travis? Didn't he get expelled from school last week?" I asked before Boone opened the basement door.

"Yeah, my moms went to his school and raised a lot of hell about it, so they let him back into Central."

When we entered the basement, Niddy and I both stopped in our tracks in total shock at what we saw. There were enough weapons on Boone's bed to fight a small army. There were at least fifteen pistols and four assault rifles.

"Damn, dog, you tatted up like you going to war or something," I said, after marveling at the rifles.

"Not unless I have to. I'm putting this network together; you two want to get down?"

"It depends on what we actually getting down with," I said. "What are you trying to do, Boone?"

"I'm arming the workers I have, but I need more because my business is picking up," Boone said as he opened his closet door.

Boone came out of the closet with a large black duffel bag. He slid the guns over and took out a large Ziploc bag full of rock cocaine. "This is a new drug called rock cocaine; we call it rocks for short. It's going to put our hood on the map. Those Rich Boys think we broke and don't have shit, but the money these rocks are going to make us is going to make our hood richer than anybody," Boone said with confidence.

He passed the Ziploc bag to Niddy, and we both looked at it. We wanted to tell Boone about the classroom incident but realized it was far less important than what he was saying, so we did not bring it up. If what Boone was saying was possible, then the PAs would have a money source the hood didn't have before. We smiled at each other after looking at the drugs; we both knew this was the beginning of making major money in the hood.

"Where are you selling it at?" I asked. "Here?"

"Hell no. You should know me better than that, Rich Boy."

"Don't call me that, Boone; I hate it when people call me that."

"I'm just fucking with you, dog, nothing to get mad about."

But I *was* mad. I considered myself a PA to the fullest and expected to be treated that way. I never cared for the Rich Boy perception of me or the talk of my family's overexaggerated wealth. When someone from the crew called me that, I felt unaccepted.

"So what's up? You two want to put in some work?" Boone asked, already knowing the answer.

We nodded in agreement and smiled, knowing this was the beginning of getting paid in the hood. After we agreed, Boone gave us both $200 worth of the drug and told us to bring him back $150.

"Whatever you do, don't sell it at school, just on the streets; mostly grown-ups use this shit, so keep some heat and be careful," he said and walked us to the door.

We left Boone's house full of confidence, and thoughts of brand-new things were already on our minds. "We about to get paid and get fresh, boy," Niddy said.

violence was occurring. Everyone was just in a good mood and ready to eat.

When the lunch matrons finally opened the doors for everyone to enter, the students quickly rushed in and got in line. The lunchroom held two hundred kids, but it was more crowded today because some kids were skipping class. Most of the kids paid for their lunch at the end of the snack bar. The low-income kids from the ghetto, though, used meal cards. Some kids laughed at the meal card kids. They ridiculed them, calling them poor and calling their meal cards food stamps. Most of the PAs had a meal card, but none of them used them lately. The recent drug selling gave them no need. Boone was leading the way as every PA in the hood was selling what the news media was calling crack cocaine.

Uddia, Z-ooh, Ant-Nice, and Sid-Money joined Niddy and me at a table. But before they sat down, Uddia made two square kids get up and leave. It was like that with all the gangs; you didn't sit at a gang's table unless you were invited. If a new kid didn't know where to sit in the lunchroom, the consequences could be devastating.

The Eight Mile Smurfs and a few members from the original Eight Mile Sconie gang had the largest crew in the lunchroom. Only the Six Mile LAs had numbers close to theirs. The group sat at two long connecting tables in the middle of the lunchroom. Rick, one of the Six Mile leaders, sat at the head of the table; he was the most dangerous member of the group. The seventeen-year-old senior sold drugs in his neighborhood and was known to have had shoot-outs with the Seven and Eight Mile Gangs when he was just twelve years old. His three-year stay in Mumford, however, had been a quiet one. His gang, like the Sevens, never had the numbers to battle with the Eights, so they stayed low key and only fought occasionally. This year, though, Rick's toughest fighter, Bloka, finally made it to Mumford. He was a sixteen-year-old freshman who should have entered high school two years ago. He and Rick were so involved in street activities that he had failed a few grade levels over the years.

Bloka was the last member from the Six Mile Gang to make it to the table; he held up the line while he ordered extra food. When he finish ordering, he walked past the Seven Mile Gang's table and noticed there were only twelve members there. Bloka then mobbed past the Eights' table, carrying his food tray with one hand and holding his nuts with the other. He aggressively stared their table down when he walked by, intimidating a few of them with his large size. He weighed more than two hundred and fifty pounds, ranking him behind Uddia as the second biggest kid in the lunchroom. He was notably strong. Most of the Eights didn't like him, because he was known for terrorizing some of the Eight Mile kids on their own block. The Six Mile Gang was much more aggressive in the streets than they were in Mumford.

"I'm ready to scrap with any of them fools," Bloka said after sitting down next to Rick.

"Look, I want everybody to stay on they guard," Rick said. "The Eights and the Sevens are beefing strong, but remember we got beefs with both of them."

"You right about one thing, Rick," Stan said. "The beef is strong between the Eights and the Sevens, but I don't think we have to worry about the Sevens; hell, we haven't fought them in over a year now."

"Stan got a point, Rick; the Sevens basically live on the border of our hood, and we don't even beef with them in the streets," Bloka said as he devoured the last of his food.

Stan was also a senior and an intelligent one. Rick had depended on many of his suggestions during their whole tenure in Mumford. He was often misjudged by his adversaries. Kids who had never seen him fight figured that he couldn't, a mistake that usually cost anyone who tried him. Not only was he a fighter, he was a good one.

"Give me some numbers, Stan, starting with us."

"It's twenty-one of us, Rick, and it's twenty-five to maybe thirty of them Eights, and that's not including their girlfriends. There's no other gang in the lunchroom with numbers like that."

"Twenty-one," Rick said excitedly and then looked for himself by analyzing the table. "That's almost our whole crew in the school!"

While Rick discussed their unusually high number, the Eights were a couple of tables over, stewing about Bloka's disrespect. It was rare for anyone to diss the Eights, let alone a table full of them. Billy and Clyde had been sitting next to Bam-Bam and Frog when Bloka had walked by holding his nuts, and all of them were fuming. Everyone at the table knew if it got out in the hood what he had done, they would be laughed at for not retaliating. Billy and Clyde came to the conclusion that they would have to attack Bloka, and it would have to be done this lunch hour.

Black Mike, Romeo, and P-Coal had observed the Bloka scenario before they sat down and knew there was going to be some trouble.

"Man, it's about to be some shit. You see how them Eights start huddling up after Bloka walked past them like that?" P-Coal said, with obvious concern.

"Yeah, but that's their fight, not ours; I have no love for a Six or Eight," Romeo replied.

"Me neither, but the LAs are deep this hour; let's see how this turn out," Black Mike said with interest.

While the Seven Mile Gang looked on, Bloka and Stan left their table and headed toward the large garbage can near the food stand. Billy and the whole Eight Mile Gang stared at them fiercely when they passed their table again. Even though Bloka and Stan ignored them and continued to walk toward the garbage can, they both knew they were walking through a danger zone. Suddenly, Billy and Clyde left their seats with violence on their mind. They cut off the walking lane and motioned six other members to cut off the other lane back to Bloka and Stan's table.

They didn't notice the Eights till they turned away from the garbage can, and then they walked down the lane Billy and Clyde had blocked. As the four faced off in the middle of the lane, Stan gasped when he noticed four more Eights plus the six other members coming like a steamroller behind them. But Bloka's speed was uncanny. He viciously chopped Clyde in the face with one of his large hands and staggered him with more body chops. As Clyde fell to his knees, Stan and Billy wrestled and rolled over a table onto the other side on the floor. Just before the fast-moving Eight Mile Gang reached Stan, Bloka picked Clyde up and slammed him into the others as he went over the table. The body-slam caused four of them to fall down over each other in the lane, blocking the others behind them.

The other Eight Mile members joined the fray. "Eight o'clock, eight o'clock," they chanted, while the matrons and the two lunchroom truant officers ran out. The truant officers didn't run out because they were scared, they ran out to get help. There was no way two people could stop the brawl. "Six o'clock, six o'clock," Rick chanted, as he led the whole Six Mile Gang toward the Eights. Everybody who wasn't part of the fighting cleared out of the way and ran out of the lunchroom. Others stood against the walls watching like they were at a boxing match.

"Man, I bet you a bottle of ole 'E' the LAs going to win this one, Uddia," Ant-Nice said, after seeing Bloka body-slam two more kids.

"That's a bet, fool," Uddia replied, shaking his hand to make the wager legit.

Even though Uddia disliked the Eight Mile Gang, he had never seen them lose a gang fight in Mumford.

"I think I'm going to side up with Uddia on this one, Ant. It's going to take more LAs than that to stop the Eights," I said.

Meanwhile, the Six Mile Gang appeared to be winning big, as Rick and Bloka led the fight. Bloka was easily doing the most damage. He knocked Clyde and four other Eights out of the fight, giving confidence to his crew. Bloka's onslaught prompted Clyde and Billy's girlfriends, Sharon and Janet, to join the fight. They had stayed seated when the fight had started, but now they led five other girls into the battle. They picked up chairs and attacked their enemies from the back. The sneak attacks took out three LAs before they realized the girls had joined the fight. The girls' wild attacks caught the Six Mile Gang clearly by surprise. Sharon was relentless as she struck Six Mile Jim with a chair, over and over. He became another victim of their onslaught, falling to the ground unconscious. The beating didn't stop there, as she continued to strike him after he was down. Then Rick came out of nowhere and punched Sharon in the eye, sending her crashing to the floor. When Bam-Bam and Frog saw that, they made their way toward Rick.

Bam-Bam and Frog were considered leaders and personal advisors to the up-and-coming Smurfs, but they had seen enough when Sharon went down. Bam-Bam was short and stocky and an excellent fighter, while Frog was almost as big as Bloka. Eight Six Mile members were left against fourteen Eight Mile Smurfs when the two joined the fight. The two-to-one odds favored the Eights, as the much fresher Frog and Bam-Bam started striking some of the tired LAs with hard body blows. Bloka's fatigue was more evident as the wild fighting was taking a toll on him. He stopped swinging for a moment and covered up his body with his large arms till he recovered his strength.

Rick and Stan yelled, "Six minutes, six minutes," and all the LAs ran from their individual battles to them. Then they jammed up together and formed a tight circle. The planned procedure for an outnumbered situation was meant to cover them when they fought. Bloka was the only one who didn't make it to the circle. He had fought so deep into the Eights' crew he was too far away to rejoin his friends. He fought like a warrior trying to make it through but was cut off by Frog. Everyone in the school had imagined a fantasy match between the two young gangsters from day one. Now the most anticipated fight in the school was about to become reality.

Frog was the first to strike; he hit Bloka with an overhand right to the jaw and then followed it up with left and right hooks to his midsection. But Bloka was much stronger and tougher than Frog anticipated. He withstood the onslaught and struck Frog in the face with numerous straight jabs that left both his eyelids swollen. Frog retaliated from that with a well-placed kick to Bloka's stomach, and then he continued to punch his stomach. The idea was to wear the young giant down, but it was going to take more than some hard body blows to defeat Bloka. He shook off Frog's body attack, went low twice, and came back up high with two vicious uppercuts to his chin. Frog stumbled and staggered backward but somehow managed to stay on his feet.

While the two young gangsters fought like hell, Rick and the Six Mile circle was starting to falter. The long fight and the Eights' numbers were wearing thin on the group, as the circle fell from seven members to five. Meanwhile, Black Mike and P-Coal ordered two of their members to lock the lunchroom doors with mops and broomsticks in between the handles. They knew that sooner or later the truant officers were going to return with the police. Onlookers who stood against the walls nervously watched as the youngsters locked the doors. Then the unthinkable happened: Black Mike stood up out of his chair and chanted, "Seven up, seven up," and twelve members from Seven Mile Road rose up from their tables and joined the fight. The students who had stayed to watch a good fight suddenly had second thoughts and wished they had left earlier when they had the chance.

The four leaders from Seven Mile, Black Mike, P-Coal, Romeo, and Hash, led the charge against the very surprised Eight Mile Gang. The four leaders bum-rushed Frog from the back, while the other Sevens attacked the Eights. Black Mike and the others had always discussed a possible alliance with their neighborhood rivals. But there was always some kind of beef in the streets that kept that from happening. "Seven up," Black Mike chanted as four Seven Mile girls got involved and attacked Janet and Pam, the last two Eight Mile girls standing.

"Cat fight in the house!" Z-ooh yelled.

"Fuck that bitch up!" Uddia said loudly, as the violence got closer to the PAs against the wall. The girls were struck by so many blows from the four Seven Mile girls that they collided with each other and fell side by side. The Eight girls followed that with wild kicks to their bodies that left Janet and Pam screaming for their life.

Just a few feet away, Bam-Bam was holding off an LA member and a Seven Mile member with a chair like his very life depended on it. He heard the screams from the girls but had to fight on or face the same fate as them. While he continued to swing the chair on his attackers, Frog was being engulfed by punches coming from everywhere. The four leaders from Seven Mile were laying it on him so badly, Bloka stopped swinging and watched in awe. The well-placed punches put him in a daze before he finally fell to the floor. "Yeah, this is for the clothesline you gave me, fool," Black Mike said, and he kicked the fallen kid three more times. There was so much hysteria in the lunchroom, nobody had noticed the doors bucking in and out.

The few LAs who were left standing gained new life when the Seven Mile Gang joined the fight. They broke from the defensive circle and helped beat down the rest of the Eight Mile Gang, all except for Bam-Bam, who was still holding kids back with a chair.

The police finally broke into the lunchroom; when they saw Bam-Bam holding the chair in a striking position, they threw him to the floor and handcuffed him. Other officers took out their clubs and waved them around like swords, daring the others to get violent. The move was a scare tactic that was normally used to keep wannabe gangsters and thugs in line on the streets.

"I want everyone that's injured to stay here and wait for the ambulance," said Officer Jones. "Everyone else, leave the lunchroom and go to class."

The lunchroom was a bloody mess. It was the first time in Mumford history the Eight Mile Gang had lost a big fight. But they weren't the only losers, as Officers Brooks and Jones looked over the injured kids from each gang.

"Man, I can't believe this shit, Ted," Brooks said. "We got rid of every dangerous weapon in the school, and this happens."

"Not all the weapons, Steve," Jones said. "Look!" He pointed to one kid who was wearing brass knuckles.

ass till the Sevens got involved. They caught us off guard, and we just couldn't recover."

"You mean the Sevens and the Sixes are together now?" Moe asked, surprised.

"Right! I didn't see it coming. I should have known those two gangs were going to click up sooner or later, especially since we've been whipping both their asses in school for years."

"We need to have a meeting," Moe said. "Leaders only. Meet me at the park when everybody gets out of school."

"That's a bet."

Bam-Bam hung the phone up and went to his leather seat, but before he sat down, the phone rang again.

"Hello?"

"Hello baby, how are you doing?"

"What's up, Venus? You miss me?" Bam-Bam asked after recognizing the sweet sound of her voice.

"Look baby, I don't have but a few minutes to talk. I just want to let you know the Sevens and Sixes are having a party tonight in the Six Mile hood. It starts at nine o'clock. I thought you might want to know that after what happen in the lunchroom last week."

"Thanks baby, that's all I needed to hear," he said and then hung up the phone.

Meanwhile, about four miles away on Puritan Avenue, my friends and I were having fun in the candy store. We went there as soon as we got out of school to play the arcade machines. It attracted thugs from the Puritan and Fenkle area, but it was known to be the PAs' main hangout. Roni and I had bought candy from the store at the tender ages of four and six years old. Today we were having a ball playing Defender, the hottest new video game; kids basically stood in line to play it. Sometimes, Roni and I would save a quarter all day just to play the game.

"Hey Roni," I said, "I heard you've been fucking kids up at your new school."

"Hell yeah," he said. "I had to knock a few chumps out because I fucked their hoes."

"You need to cool out with that shit, Roni, you know how these fools are about their females."

"You know me better than anyone, Muscles; you know I don't give a fuck; if the bitch gives me the eye, I'm trying to fuck her," he said, which brought laughter from Niddy and Uddia.

Roni was one of the youngest PAs, but he probably had the biggest heart in the group. He would talk shit to anyone and would fight just the same. I was two years older than him, but I always treated him like we were the same age. We had fought many times together and felt no one could beat us. Everyone in the Puritan area knew how close we were. But I always worried about Roni's temper; he was a ticking bomb ready to go off at any time. His local beefs were making life dangerous, and his don't-give-a-fuck attitude was bringing us too much attention. Not even his cousin Niddy could control him.

The candy storecandy store was like a dance club; kids danced to the latest songs that boomed from three large speakers. It was the place to be if you were young and poor and wanted to have fun in the hood. Big Mike, the owner of the store, approached me while I was playing Defender with Roni.

"Muscles, you got a phone call in my office," Big Mike said. "Look, I don't care about you kids using my phone, but if you're on it longer than two minutes, I'm going to charge you for it. This is a business phone, not the PAs' phone."

When I entered the office, Big Mike gave me the phone and then left to give me some privacy.

"Hello? What up, Moe? I should of figure it was you. Big Mike wouldn't even have come and got me if you weren't my cousin." I paused. "What can I do for you?"

"You know that hardware I let you borrow for a rainy day?"

"Yes," I said.

"Well, I need it in the next hour, can it happen?" he asked urgently.

"Of course it can happen, but you got to come and get it. There's no way I can make it to Eight Mile in an hour."

"All right, that's a bet."

I hung up the phone and went back to the arcade games in the front of the store. Ironically, as soon as I got there, Z-ooh, Robin, and Sid-Money were just coming inside. "PA down," the three chanted heartily.

"All right, you kids, keep it down! I'm running a business here, not a pep rally," Big Mike said with authority. Whenever Big Mike yelled, everyone listened; it was simple as that. He demanded respect in the store and got it with no arguments.

Youngsters started crowding the store as teenagers arriving from school couldn't wait to play the arcade games. There were about thirty-five kids inside the store and twenty-five more hanging around outside. About a third of those kids were Puritan girls. The situation with the girls across Puritan was another story. They were poor and considered ghetto and too street for some Rich Boys. Most girls from the Puritan area dated boys from their own neighborhood and rarely ventured elsewhere. This was how it was in every hood on the west side of Detroit; naturally, no one dated outside their hood. There was almost certain to be an altercation if someone traveled to another hood for a date. Not because of jealousy or anything like that; it was because of the large volume of gang fighting in each hood.

Niddy greeted the three PAs at the door with love and daps as everyone danced to the music. He checked his pockets and pulled out eighty dollars, flashing it in the air, and said, "Yeah boy, I made a killing last night; I got a fat ass knot!"

I smiled at Niddy's boast. Everyone knew he was a braggart at times, but he spoke the truth. Niddy and I were making good money selling drugs at night. Crack was quickly becoming the most sought-after drug in the street. We saved our money so we could spend lavishly at the malls on the weekend.

I checked my customized gold watch I had bought from a rock head last night. I had given the old fool only three rocks for it. I stuck my head out the door to see if Moe was out there, and then a strong gust of wind struck me in the face. The wind sent me back in the candy storecandy store with tears in my eyes. It was October and becoming cold in Detroit. Everyone wore thick jackets and coats. Unlike the Eight Mile Gang, who loved to wear the new styled Army coat, I wore an old faded-out Army coat. The coat was long, and right now I was hiding Moe's baby Uzi inside it.

"Hey Roni," I said, "follow me outside, dog; I got a joint!"

Roni followed me out of the candy storecandy store while the others continued to play the games and dance with the girls. We walked behind the store, where everyone kicked it when they drank and smoke. I fired up a joint, hit it twice, and then passed it to Roni.

"I'm waiting on Moe to come and get his killing machine," I said. "This is where he gave it to me at, and this is where he's getting it back."

"You sound like you don't want to give it back," Roni said after choking on the weed.

"No, it's not that. It's the reason why I'm giving it back that's bothering me. Moe is about to do something stupid. I know it. He wouldn't ask for the spray gun unless he was about to use it."

Just as I said that, a taxicab pulled up behind the candy store, shining its lights on us. We knew it was Moe. He got out of the cab like someone on a mission and joined us behind the store. Moe was slender but had a bold, dangerous look to him that most kids respected on sight.

"What up, Muscles? What up, Roni? I wish I could stay and kick the shit, but I'm on a move right now. You got that for me, cuz?"

"Yeah, I got it right here," I said, handing Moe the Uzi.

"I appreciate you keeping it for me, cuz; I got to go now, that cab is waiting for me. You and Roni be careful," he said, walking back to the waiting cab.

Roni and I finished the tail end of the joint and walked back in the candy store, good and high off the strong reefer. I couldn't shake the feeling that something was wrong with Moe, something he wasn't telling me. *It was always that way with him,* I thought. *Moe would never tell you what he's done or what he's about to do.* But I planned to find out what was going on.

5

Three blocks north of Six Mile Road, kids were dancing in the street. Most of them were teenage girls practicing the latest dance moves for the party at Stan's house that night. Others were getting high and discussing the new alliance between the Sixes and Sevens, and also talking about buying 76ers jackets to represent the new partnership. Stan's house was in the middle of the block. It was an upper middle class neighborhood a couple of miles from the ghetto. Stan had a lavish lifestyle, which was why they called him "Stan the Man." Both his parents worked at General Motors and made thirty-five thousand a year each. His parents were very particular about how they lived, ate, and dressed. Stan

was having the party because his parents were out of town.

While the kids waited impatiently for the party to begin, Rick and Stan were getting high in Stan's mother's car in his driveway. They relaxed in the all-leather luxury vehicle, mesmerized in thoughts about the party that was about to jump off. Stan had planned the party weeks ago, but Rick invited Seven Mile members to show appreciation for their lunchroom intro.

"I talked to Black Mike, and they're coming just before the party jumps off," Rick said, then he finished the tail end of the joint.

"Well, you know me," Stan said. "I stay prepared. Everything's set up and ready: the music, the drinks, the whole works."

"Good, Stan, very good; I want everything to be tight when they show up. It's not every day we mingle with outsiders."

"Hey Rick, what you think about that girl you knocked out during the lunchroom fight? You think she's going to be all right?"

"Man, I don't give a fuck about that hoe. She should have kept her fine ass on the side. She took out two of my friends right in front of me. There was no way I was going to watch her take out another one."

Stan had known Rick a long time and always knew how cold and calculated he could be, but he also knew deep down that the incident bothered him. His friend caught a lot of flack from school officials after an anonymous letter said Rick was responsible for the girl's critical injuries. Officers Jones and Brooks interrogated him, but they had no solid evidence; all they could do was hope for a confession. Rick didn't budge, though, and they were forced to let him go. He'd been on edge ever since.

Stan sprayed his mother's car out, and then the two went into Stan's large brick house high and geeked about the fun they were going to have at their party. After they walked inside, kids down the street started making their way toward Stan's house.

Meanwhile, Romeo, Black Mike, and Hash were just pulling up in P-Coal's driveway. "Hash, go and tell P-Coal and Cowboy to come out so we can get to the party early," Black Mike ordered, blowing his horn twice. Before Hash got out of the car, the two were already coming outside, accompanied by Jerry. They all jammed into the back of the car. Romeo and Black Mike glared at Jerry as he entered the car. The two leaders didn't like him because he was not actually a member. Jerry had moved into a Seven Mile neighborhood last summer and started attending Mumford this year. He was going with Cowboy's sister Tammy, which got him in good with the Seven Mile Gang. She was highly sought after by Romeo and Black Mike, another reason why they didn't like him. But Cowboy, who was probably the most popular member, thought Jerry was cool and willed him into the group.

"I talked to Tim before I left, he should be meeting us at Stan's house around the same time we get there," Cowboy said, breaking the silence in the car. Tim was coming to the party with Black Mike's cousin Lee and two other members. They had been selected by Black Mike himself to watch their backs while they mingled at the party. The two cars showed up at Stan's house at the same time. They all got out of their cars and walked uneasily to the porch. They knew they were taking a dangerous chance going to a Six Mile member's house, even though they had been invited. It was the Six Mile LAs' hood, and they knew it.

Romeo heard music as he rang the bell; he wondered if the party had already started. Black Mike heard the driveway gate open; when they turned around, they were shocked to see five large kids standing in front of the gate like bodyguards. Nobody had noticed them when they walked up; they seemed to appear out of thin air. The two groups of kids stared grimly at each other until Stan appeared at the door with Rick and Bloka.

The three LAs greeted Black Mike and his friends on the porch with hugs, daps, and high fives and then led them all into the house. They all noticed how well furnished Stan's house was.

Bloka handed out rolled-up joints to Black Mike and his boys as they continued to walk through the large house.

Stan led them to the backyard, where the party was getting under way. Black Mike and his friends were stunned at the setup in Stan's backyard. The patio was set up with a platform like a stage, where two DJs operated large mixers and other music equipment.

They walked through the patio with amazement but were even more surprised when they walked into the yard. There were about fifty chairs circled neatly around the yard, leaving a very large space in the middle. The garage was set up for recreational needs, with arcade games and a pool table; dice games were already under way as kids started coming into the yard from the driveway gate. If you were from the Six Mile hood, the party was the place to be tonight. There were already forty members from the neighborhood in the yard, and many more were expected to come before the night was out. The five armed soldiers on duty were patrolling the gate. Black Mike and his boys were also armed, but there were no beefs and no altercations, as kids were having the time of their lives.

The weather was surprisingly mild, causing many youngsters to take off their jackets and coats. They were high and hot from dancing intensely. Rick, Stan, and Black Mike walked to the front of the yard with five pretty girls from the party. They laughed and talked with them while the five soldiers at the gate looked on.

Meanwhile, a few blocks away, three masked gunmen were parked in front of a vacant house. They were heavily armed in an old Chrysler, and another car full of masked kids was parked behind them. Both cars pulled away and drove slowly toward Stan's house with their lights off. The loud music from the party drowned out their engines as the cars approached the house. Rick and two pretty girls, Angela and Donna, were sitting on the couch swings in the middle of the yard when the first car came into view.

"Everybody get down now!" Black Mike yelled at the top of his lungs. "That car is about to spit."

Unfortunately, his warning was too late. The first car jerked to a stop, and two masked kids hung out the windows and started blasting. One gunman unloaded a whole clip on the five soldiers at the gate, dropping three of them instantly. None of the guards had a chance to raise their pistols. Black Mike and Stan hit the dirt as soon as the shots were fired. The other gunman unloaded a fully automatic Uzi on Rick and the two girls. Every bullet seemed to hold their bodies up as they jerked uncontrollably from the barrage. He rotated his killing machine from left to right until it was empty, and the car peeled out from in front of the house like it was never there. Smoke and burnt rubber still lingered in the air from the first car when the second one came on the scene. Masked gunmen got out that car and fired Mack tens and elevens at Stan's house. Everyone in the front and in the backyard ran for shelter when they heard the second car squeal to a stop. Black Mike and Stan took refuge under his mother's car with pistols out, hoping to get a good shot, but they wisely decided not to shoot. The gunmen had no intentions of shooting anyone. Instead, they unloaded their killing machines on Stan's house, leaving it riddled with bullets. After shooting the house up, the masked gunmen walked slowly back to the car and yelled out the infamous Eight Mile slogan, "Eight o'clock," before the car sped off.

The sounds of moans and crying filled the air, muffling out the faint sounds of sirens. The five soldiers who were shot at the gate had been hit hard, but none of them had life-threatening injuries. However, the two girls who had been struck by a rain of bullets were already dead before they fell to the ground. Surprisingly, Rick was still alive, as he grimaced from the many gunshots that had hit him. Small streams of blood came down the side of his mouth when he screamed. He tried to get up but couldn't move; in fact, every time he tried to get up, it got blurrier and blurrier. Then two blurry faces approached him as he lay drained by the effort from trying to get up. The pain Rick was feeling caused him to pass out before he could identify the blurry faces. If he had stayed conscious longer, he would have seen it was Stan and Black Mike trying to revive him.

"Don't die on me, homey," Stan said. "The ambulance is on its way, baby, just hold on, dog, just hold on." He held his bloody friend while Bloka and the rest of the Six Mile Gang ran to his side. The sounds of police and ambulance sirens got louder and louder, which put Black Mike and his boys in an awkward position.

"Stan, baby, I hope Rick makes it," he said, "but we got to bell up out of here, dog, before the cops arrive." He put his hand firmly on Stan's shoulder when he rose up. "He'll be fine, dog, just fine; give me a call and let me know how he's doing. Sorry I got to leave like this," he said, and then he and his friends hurried from the scene through the growing crowd.

Black Mike left in his car full of anger, with revenge obviously on his mind, but he knew now was the time to squat and think. As far as Black Mike was concerned, the Eight Mile Gang had taken their wars in the streets to a whole new level.

Monday morning after the three-day weekend was very memorable. The two pretty girls who had gotten killed were from Mumford, and their deaths made front page news. Rick had been on the brink of death but pulled through after being rushed to the hospital. He had been shot twenty-two times, and doctors spent hours removing the shells from his body. The killings at Stan's house were being talked about all over the streets and the school, and rumors were already starting to surface. Many thought Bam-Bam and

Frog were responsible for the shooting because of the fight in the lunchroom; others thought the untrustworthy Sevens had set them up.

First hour ended and I was on my way to meet Jerry on the first floor by the girls' bathroom. He had called me over the weekend and said he had to meet me. As I walked, I thought about when we had first met in the third grade; we had been friends ever since. I hadn't seen him since our meeting on the first day of school. I wondered what was so urgent that we had to meet like this.

"What's up, homey?" he asked when he saw me in the hall. "How is your family?"

"They're doing fine, Jerry, just fine. So tell me, homey, what the hell you got to say here that you couldn't say on the phone?"

"Well, when I seen you last month, I didn't get a chance to tell you where I moved to. I live on Seven Mile now."

"Yeah, you were saying something about that on the phone. Is that the hood you're claiming now, dog, or are you just laying your head there?"

"Both, dog, both. Ever since they invited me to that party a few nights ago, the Sevens have been showing me nothing but love. That's what I wanted to holler at you about. The Sevens and Sixes have hooked up, dog, we're the Seventy-Sixers now. Everybody from both hoods is getting down, so what's up with you? You're from Six Mile Road and known in the hood. You want to get down?"

"Down with who? The LAs and the Sevens?"

"Hell yeah, dog, I could hook you up with them. I been getting high with some of the top leaders, and I've been mentioning your name, dog," Jerry said as if he was actually doing me a favor.

I eyed Jerry angrily.

"What? What the fuck you do that for, dog? How the hell can you ask me something like that? You know I'm down with the PAs for life," I said sharply.

"Man, you still fucking with them broke-ass bums from across Puritan? I told you way back, hanging with them poor fools going to bring you down," he said. "You need to—"

I rudely cut him off.

"You're stepping out of line, Jerry. You're my boy and all, but I'm not going to stand here and let you diss my other homeys. I grew up with them like I grew up with you; rich or poor; we are to be reckoned with."

After I said that, Jerry knew there was no way I would even consider joining the Seventy-Sixers.

"All right, dog, do what you do, but I'm telling you, the Seventy-Sixers are about to take over this whole school, whether you're down with us or not."

"They may have taken over you, but nobody's taking over the PAs!" I paused for a moment and then continued, "All I can do if our crew ever clashes with your crew is prevent my boys from fucking with you, dog; unfortunately, I can't say the same for your boys." I paused again and stared at my watch. "Well, I got to go now or I'll be late for my second hour; we'll talk more about this. Peace," I said coldly and then left the scene.

As I walked to class, I couldn't shake the feeling that Jerry was in grave danger. He was never really a fighter or banger in my eyes, and I felt he faced more of a problem with his own crew than anybody else.

One hour passed, and Bloka was on his way to third hour class by himself. It was the only stretch of the day he had to walk alone. Normally, he wouldn't have given a damn if he walked alone or not; he was known for fighting by himself. But the situation was different now. After the killings at Stan's party, Stan had taken over as Mumford's Six Mile leader and ordered many Six Mile soldiers to accompany him to every class. They were precautions against gangs who may want to strike at their leadership in the school. He knew Bloka could handle himself pretty well and felt no danger would come about in that short period of time. Bloka, though, grimaced at the thought of Stan's weak decisions. He didn't agree with Stan in the past, and he sure as hell didn't agree with him now. He personally thought the crew was in trouble with Stan in command and thought he was stupid for hogging up all the soldiers to walk with him. It wasn't because Bloka was scared, because he was far from that; he knew walking alone in the halls during a beef with the Eights was very dangerous. The hallways were crowded as he walked through them, thinking about how hard the Eights had hit them when they had taken out Rick. The LAs depended on him for numerous things, and leading them into battle was one of them.

Bloka's thoughts of Rick disappeared when Venus, a fine, pretty girl, approached him with a smile.

"Bloka, Bloka," she said, giving him a big hug in the middle of the hallway. "Where you been, baby? Why don't you call me? We haven't talked since I moved last year; I know you still got my number." She embraced him once more.

"Yeah, it's been a minute," he said. "So how you been doing, you still live on the west side?"

Her only response was the pretty smile that went hand and hand with her beauty. She then grabbed his hand and led him down the hallway.

"Come to my locker, baby, I got something to show you," she said, flashing her shiny white teeth as she smiled.

While the two walked, Bloka noticed me walking in the same direction and staring at them. He knew me from the hood and never beefed with me, so he ignored my stares and continued to walk with Venus. Any other time, he probably would have confronted me for staring at him like that. It was obvious he was excited to see Venus, and he sure wasn't about to let anything spoil that. Even though they never dated, he called her his little princess and was always protective of her.

"Damn, she got a lot of ass," he said, after feeling her booty.

Then she abruptly pushed him away and ran down the crowded hallway. He looked confused until he heard me yell, "Bloka! Look out!" But my warning was futile, as four Eights attacked him. They each struck him with punches to a different area in his midsection like the blows were choreographed. He covered himself up with his massive arms and backed up against the lockers; five more Eights ran to the scene. They attacked him the same way, and the sequence of punches slightly dazed the young giant as he used the lockers to hold himself up and safeguard his back. Since most of the kids he was facing were lightweight freshmen, their punches had little effect on him. The fact that they were so small made Bloka feel he was unstoppable, because he was still standing. He was in a psycho mode like a cornered animal; he started throwing haymakers off the lockers like a madman.

I watched in amazement as the fight became gruesome. I couldn't believe Bloka was still standing and fighting the Eights by himself like that. He was doing so well that I was tempted to help him. But I knew I would be out of place if I did, so I remained a spectator like everyone else. As I watched, Bloka picked up one of the Smurfs and rammed him into three of his friends with a thrust of power so explosive, his momentum sent all four of them crashing into the wall.

That bitch is going to pay for setting me up, he thought as the uphill battle shifted down the hallway. Billy and Clyde came to the scene, swinging at Bloka like they never swung before. The flurry of punches startled him as two other Smurfs grabbed both his legs, attempting to bring the giant down. However, it was like trying to bring down an elephant. He ignored the two at his legs and continued throwing mind-staggering haymakers. After creating enough room to function, he pounded the two at his legs, blow after blow, till neither was moving.

Suddenly, just when it seemed like he might prevail with three more down, seven more Smurfs came to the scene. They all attacked him at once, sending his body crashing backward into the lockers by the study hall. For the first time in the battle, Bloka was off balance. Each Smurf struck him again and again against the lockers; he began to get dizzy, but he did not fall. The spectators watched in awe as Bloka was determined to stay on his feet. It was something never seen before in the Mumford halls. Punches that didn't have an effect on him earlier started to take their toll, as he managed to free himself from the lockers. Smurf after Smurf attacked him with punches everywhere he turned. He swung frantically at his attackers, fearing he was about to fall, and then like angels from the sky, the truant officers stormed the hallways, saving him from further punishment. They tried to apprehend his attackers but only managed to run them off.

"Are you okay, son?" they asked as they walked to the principal's office.

The truant officers called for an ambulance, as students stood in total shock over Bloka's victims. Five were unconscious, and three more were injured. The Smurfs had the last laugh, though, as tears ran down the young giant's cheeks from the pain when he entered the principal's

Meanwhile, Frog and ten Smurfs were mobbing the halls just when the bell rang. Ever since the killings at the party, the popularity of his gang had grown. No one actually knew who did the shooting, but most speculated that Frog and the Eights at least knew who did it. Frog walked with a swagger, knowing Bloka was out of the school, but he still wanted revenge. "I wish I could've have gone one more round with that fool," he said as he and his boys reached the neutral bathroom. They entered the bathroom chanting their Eight Mile slogan. Once they got everyone's attention, Frog walked to the middle of the bathroom like he was on stage. It was on his mind to shake up the school and let other gangs know that the Eights now ruled the school.

"If you're not from Eight Mile, get the fuck out the bathroom, and get the fuck out now!" he said with authority.

Black Mike and his boys were already preparing to leave, so they left without a word. Black Frost and the two Linwood Boys left also, but Uddia, Niddy, and I continued smoking in the back, ignoring Frog. Frog took this as disrespect and approached us, fuming with anger.

"You fools must be deaf or something! This is Eight Mile business, so get the fuck out before you idiots get bum-rushed in this motherfucker!"

"You don't run the neutral zone," Uddia said. "You people run the bathroom upstairs." He threw the roach he had been smoking onto the floor and balled his fists.

"We run everything, you fat motherfucker, and you going to see that if you don't get the fuck up out of here!"

The odds were against us as Uddia stood face to face with Frog, while ten of his boys stood hyped and ready for anything behind him. We didn't have any weapons, but we stood our ground like they did. The courage Uddia was displaying was just another commonality of a PA member. We never backed down, yet none of us were fools either.

"We can go head up if you want, Frog, but I know the fight won't be fair because of your boys, so we out of here, dog," Uddia said, walking away.

Uddia led Niddy and me past Frog's boys, and we left the bathroom. Frog stared at us as we left but Uddia's words echoed in his head. He already wanted revenge from the fight he had with Bloka. Before that fight, he had never lost a fight; now he thought Uddia was calling him a coward in front of his crew. Frog and his boys followed us out of the bathroom to the hallway.

"Hey fat ass, turn around so I can knock your bitch ass out!"

Uddia turned around as fast as a cat. He punched Frog with an overhand right that instantly shattered his jaw. The blow sent him tumbling backward toward the lockers. Uddia wasn't finished there, though. He followed the overhand right up with a vicious stronghold and slammed Frog into the lockers like a rag doll. Everyone stared in total amazement and backed off to give the two bangers some room. Uddia struck so fast that none of Frog's boys could react. Once he had Frog on the lockers, he started throwing haymakers that made the lockers buckle in and out. He then stepped back, as if he was marveling at his own work, and proceeded with two series of combinations. The first series of punches shattered the bones in Frog's face. The second series of punches closed both his eyes up.

Suddenly, three truant officers appeared and grabbed Uddia from the rear. They struggled with him for a minute but were able to detain him and take him into the office. Other kids walked by and gasped at what was probably the most incredible sight in school history. The severely battered Frog was encaged in a locker like he was trapped in a car wreck. He appeared to be dead as his boys started yelling for help; some tried to pull him out, with no success.

When the ambulance arrived, the paramedics carefully pried Frog out of the locker while students nervously proceeded to class. Even Niddy and I were a little worried. Retaliation was certain, we thought, as we quickly informed the rest of the gang about the new danger before we went to class. Niddy even told the Livernois PAs to crew up and be ready for anything in between the last two classes, and then he told everyone to meet up at the lockers when school ended. Uddia was sent home indefinitely. It was not the first time that Uddia had been suspended. This time, however, he had no clue about his future in Mumford.

6

On the day before Halloween, I was eating lunch with many other PAs and discussing Uddia's big fight. A week had passed by since the Uddia versus Frog debacle, and during that week tension had grown between the Eights and the PAs. Many of the Eights were angered when they had heard that Uddia would be allowed back in the school. A teacher had seen the whole fight and told the principal that Frog had started it. So Uddia was permitted back but faced a permanent vacation if he was involved in any more trouble. We all ate our lunches with smiles on our faces, while the Smurfs sitting across the room had scowls on theirs. I smiled on the outside, but deep down inside I was frowning. I didn't like the new beef with the Eights. Although neither gang had made a move against each other since the fight, all I could think about was my cousin from Eight Mile. I didn't have the heart to tell Moe that I was beefing strong with his crew.

"Hey Uddia, ever since you whipped Frog, the females have been on our dicks like rock stars," Robin said. Uddia's only response was to display a confident look on his face. He knew all too well that Robin wasn't exaggerating. After his victory over Frog, the girls all over the school were coming on strong to the PAs.

"Yeah, you really showed what type of hoes those Eights were, Uddia. Hell, they didn't even try to help when they boy was clearly getting his ass whipped," said Niddy.

"Well, you could look at it two different ways, Niddy. Either they thought he was going to beat me, or they were scared shitless," Uddia said, making everyone at the table laugh.

"I think it was both. They thought their boy was going to win but got scared when you started whipping his ass," said Wee, the Livernois leader.

Wee, who sat across from me, kept a very low profile in Mumford. I really didn't know him that well. I had heard talk of him through Niddy and others. Since I had never seen Wee and his boys fight, I wondered if they really could. As Niddy and Uddia looked on, I asked Wee the question that had been on my mind since I became a PA.

"Hey Wee, I mean no disrespect, but if we had to roll with them Eights right now, even if the odds were three to one, would you and your crew run or fight?"

Wee looked at me and laughed. He always knew I had a grudge against him, he just never knew why. Now that he understood, he decided to play it out.

"What, you think we're a bunch a hoes or something? Do you think we can't handle up? You might be down with the PAs, Muscles, but I was born and raised in the hood. Believe me, I know what it means to be a PA, Rich Boy!"

My first reaction was to get up and fight Wee for calling me the unsacred word, but I didn't, basically because everything he had said was real, plus I knew I would act the same way if it was the other way around. I knew I had taken it too far by asking him if he was a coward, but I had to know the answer. I decided to leave the whole subject alone, and a cold silence at the table followed afterward.

Ant-Nice broke the silence by telling me to put our differences behind us. He then looked at Uddia with a crazy look on his face and said, "Hey Uddia, you ready for tonight?"

Tonight was the night of all nights. It was Devil's Night. Devil's Night was a street holiday that was celebrated on the night before Halloween. Kids all over Detroit would do something devilish that night to represent the holiday. I used to participate every year, but I had stopped when the pranks had become extreme. Kids had started looting, carjacking, robbing, and hurting innocent people in the process, something I was never down with. I fought long wars in the streets, sold drugs, and was involved in a few shootouts, but I never robbed anyone or hurt innocent people.

"What about you, Muscles, you going out this year or are you chilling?" Ant-Nice asked.

"Sorry, dog, I just don't get down like that. My Devil's Night days were over with a long time ago."

"Damn, dog, you never go out. Earlier, you asked Wee a wild question; now I'm asking you one. Are you scared to go out tonight?" Z-ooh asked. He had a straight face, but I knew he was joking.

"Look, trick, if Devil's Night is your night, hey, knock yourself out, but don't knock me because I'm not going."

Z-ooh and I laughed heartily. Everyone was used to us arguing. Despite our differences, Z-ooh and I had a lot of respect for each other, although I knew he wondered how someone like me from a different hood could be so accepted by the others.

"Damn, I forgot, I start my seventh hour class today," I said angrily.

"Seventh hour? That's the most dangerous time of the day," Niddy said. "Haft the Sevens in the school hang around school that hour."

I finally crossed the road that officially took me off school property. I breathed a sigh of relief. Unfortunately, the dangers of my journey were just beginning. I anxiously lit up a cigarette to calm my nerves but never stopped walking. Now I only needed to walk two short blocks from the school to get to the bus stop.

I gently released the hammer on my gun in the bag after noticing a police car coming down the street. I tried to look as square as possible by turning my sports hat straight instead of tilted to the side like I normally wore it. The car passed, but when the bus stop came into my view, I noticed two students waiting there. I couldn't make them out, but as I got closer, I recognized Jerry.

"What up, dog? When did you get a seventh hour?" I said, when I greeted him at the stop.

"I don't have one; I'm just chilling out, dog," he replied.

"Who is your boy?"

"This is my boy Calley. Calley, this is my boy Muscles. Calley here is from California but lived most his life here in the Big D. He's down with the Sevens too," Jerry said proudly.

Calley reached out to shake my hand but I hesitated slightly. The reluctance did not go unnoticed by Jerry as he stared at me with concern on his face. My dislike of Seven Mile at the time was becoming more and more evident to Jerry, and I knew it.

"Calley and I are waiting for these bitches, dog. This is around the time they come too; I'll probably pull about four or five numbers today before we bell out. You ought to hang out here with us for a minute before you get on the bus."

"Sorry, dog, I'm bailing out of here soon as the first bus come."

I then took a clean rag out my school bag and started wiping my newly acquired gym shoes.

"What you think about my new padded leathers? They fresh, aren't they?" I asked, continuing to wipe my shoes. "I bought them over the weekend at Northland."

"Yeah, they funky fresh, dog, funky fresh, but get you some glass cleaner and spray them down, then wipe them. Watch how they shine then."

All the young gangsters, rich or poor, wore high-priced gym shoes, and the padded leather kind were at the top of everyone's list. Jerry, who loved to dress differently from anyone else, wore the candy apple red padded leather Chucks. They were the most expensive gym shoe on the market. The padded leather tens were being stolen from kids every day in Detroit. Calley was also wearing brand-new tens, except he wore the regular kind without the padded leather. Many youths thought you had to be a soldier to wear these shoes, and they were basically right, especially since squares and nerds were usually the victims. Cool-looking gym shoes were a must in high school; everyone and their momma knew the first thing a Detroit girl noticed in a guy was his shoes. In fact, some kids wouldn't even go to school if they had to go without a proper pair of kicks.

While Jerry and Calley talked, I noticed a young man with braided hair cross the street; he walked toward the bus stop. He was wearing a long trench coat and walked as though he was fighting the bristling winds itself. The closer he got, the more I thought something was very odd about the kid. Then all of a sudden, the kid pulled out a forty-four Magnum from under his coat and planted the pistol right on Calley's nose.

"Check 'em in," he said, after staring hard at Calley's gym shoes.

Without hesitation, Calley slid his feet out of the shoes like he was wearing slippers. The youngster picked up the shoes and crossed the street, getting into a car that just arrived. My first reaction was to blast the kid in the back when he turned and walked away, just for making the mistake of robbing someone and then turning his back. The only reason I didn't shoot him was because my shoes hadn't been ganked. Besides, the police had just passed by me; I would be a fool to give them a reason to come back.

"Man, did you see that shit?" Calley said. "Man, fuck that, that fool ain't about to get away with this. Jerry, let's go tell Brooks and Jones, they'll probably get my shoes back for me … are you coming?"

"Yeah, I'm coming; what about you, Muscles? You want to come with us?" Jerry asked, just as the bus was pulling up.

"Naw, dog, I got somewhere to be; besides, I don't talk to cops, dog," I said, and then I got on the bus.

I waved at the two through the windows before sitting down. I had dodged a bullet back at the bus stop. It could have easily been me that was robbed, I thought as I sat down in the back next to a large group of girls. As soon as I sat down, I made eye contact with a girl I knew from Beaubian Middle School. She had been looking at me hard the past two weeks, but I was reluctant to make a move on her, especially after seeing Bloka get set up by a girl from another neighborhood. I decided to step to the fine-looking square. The girl she was sitting next to got up, so I left my seat and sat next to her.

"How you doing, Mia? You been okay?" I said, trying to sound cool.

"Oh, now you want to speak. Boy, you see me in the halls every day and you couldn't even come give me a hug. I thought we were better than that, James," she said.

"My fault, baby, I should've step to you and gave you a hug, but since I never hugged you at Beaubian, it wasn't on my mind to attempt to. Now that you mention it, I would love to give you a hug, baby," I said, with a smile.

"Boy, you crazy," she said, blushing. She then rose up, pulled the bus cord, and said, "Only if you promise to let go, because everyone that hugs me never want to let me go."

I got up and embraced her with the strongest hug I ever gave, and then stared dead into her eyes before I let her go.

"Damn, girl, you know what I want now, don't you?"

"Yeah, now you want my number, but I don't have time to give it to you; I got to leave. You'll see me again; I enjoyed the hug, bye."

Mia walked off the bus with a swish that was so natural that every kid on the bus eyed her till she was out of sight. She was light-skinned and thick in all the right places, and her new styled jeans fitted her like a second skin. She was definitely a sight for sore eyes.

This day turned out to be all right after all, I said to myself.

A couple of hours passed since Calley got his shoes taken at the bus stop, and darkness was slowly replacing the daylight. The Seven Mile Road members were entering the Hampton Middle School playground. Hampton was a breeding school for the Seven Mile Gang, like Beaubian was for the Eight Mile Gang and Custard Elementary School was for the PA Gang. Seven Mile kids hung out at the playground during the summer or late in the evening when school was out. They usually drank a few beers, talked shit with each other, and kicked a few laughs. Today, though, the shit talking was serious. Earlier, Jerry had tried to warn Calley about going to the police and told him he wasn't going with him at the last minute. Despite Jerry's warnings, Calley went to the police anyway and gave a full description of the kid who had stolen his shoes. Now, Black Mike and other Seven Mile members were ridiculing him unmercifully for doing it.

"We heard you ran to the cops crying like a bitch because you got your shit checked in, fool. You suppose to be a Seven Mile killer. You represent us like we represent you. But you want to look like a bitch in front of the whole school about some shoes," Black Mike said angrily.

P-Coal grabbed Calley by his polo shirt, pinned him back to the monkey bars, and said, "You must think we're some bitches too."

"What's the deal, man?" Calley said. "All I did was tell the cops I got my shoes stole from me. I don't see what the big deal about it is; I didn't snitch on our gang!"

"Bitch, we don't care if they took the clothes off your motherfucking back! It was still no reason to be in a cop's face," Cowboy said bluntly.

Jerry, who was high and drunk, couldn't stop laughing about it in the background. He knew the kids were just fucking with Calley but hoped they would stop soon.

"Hey Jerry, what's up with your boy Muscles?" Romeo said. "I heard he calls himself a PA but live off Six Mile Road, what's up with that?"

"He is a PA, Romeo, and I respect him for what he is; after all, he is my friend, you know."

"Well, if your boy and those PAs ever step out of line, you know we're going to straighten them out, right?"

"Well … yeah, I presume so."

"Why you hesitated when you answered then? Are you sure you're ready for beef, boy?"

"I'm always ready for beef, Romeo, but I thought we was beefing with the Eights, not the PAs."

"We beef with anybody that's not down with us, Jerry, and you're going to see that tonight. We're going to end our alliance with the Six Mile Gang tonight, and what better night to end a friendship than on Devil's Night?"

Jerry looked concerned, and it was for good reason.

Three hours later on the other side of Six Mile, Stan and about thirty Six Mile members were hanging out in front of his house. They were all getting ready for Devil's Night, except they planned to celebrate the dreadful holiday differently this year. Instead of doing devilish pranks, they were going to visit their friend Rick at the hospital. "It's nine o'clock, time to bail," Bloka said. All thirty members then jammed into six cars and mobbed out of the hood toward the hospital.

Bloka was deep in thought while he rode in the back seat of the lead car with Stan. He really missed Mumford and felt he got dealt a bad hand before his sudden departure. He thought about how his old friend Venus had set him up, and then he smiled when he thought about the punishment she received for the dark scheme. Just days after his dismissal, Bloka had told the Six Mile girls about Venus's treachery. And the results were devastating. Shell, Niddy's girlfriend, led an all-out attack on Venus by the girls' bathroom. They stomped her so violently, when the ambulance finally arrived she was unrecognizable. Shell was one of the few girls who dated someone out of the hood. Most guys from her neighborhood didn't like it, but Bloka really didn't care. She was tall, fine, and sharper than a knife, but dangerous when it came down to violence.

The six cars arrived at the hospital at quarter after nine. They parked and entered the hospital lobby. Stan and Bloka went to the front desk and got passes for ten visitors. Stan had planned the visit; the arrangement was for thirty members to visit Rick in three different groups off one group of passes. Since there were so many of them, each group was to visit for one hour while the others chilled out in the lobby.

Stan, who led the way to Rick's room, took a deep breath before he entered. He hated hospitals; they gave him the creeps. "Rick baby, what up, homey? How you feel?" he said, walking to his bedside.

Rick was sitting straight up in his bed; the sudden entrance obviously caught him by surprise. "What up, Stan?" he said, with dryness in his tone.

Rick felt the same way about surprises that Stan did about hospitals. He hated them.

Rick's recovery was going well, though, considering they removed twenty-two bullets from his frame. There was one problem, though: he had temporarily lost the use of his legs. He was told a rehabilitation program could help him walk again one day. He took the news hard at first, but his prayers made him stronger each night. While Rick was cool and calm about it, his parents were devastated about his condition.

"Bloka baby, I heard you went out like a true trooper and fought nearly the whole Smurf gang," he said as kids crowded around his bed.

"Yeah, but I would've never been in that situation if you were in charge, Rick."

"What the fuck does that suppose to mean, Bloka? You got a problem with how I lead?" Stan retorted sharply.

Rick gave both of them a crazy look, instantly letting them know they needed to chill out.

"What you two need to do is get on the same page before the Sevens notice that you're not."

"The Sevens are down with us now, Rick; why should we have to worry about them?" said Stan.

"Because lying in this bed for three weeks gave me plenty time to think, and I think hooking up with the Sevens might not have been a good idea." He paused to adjust his pillow and then continued, "I think opening them up to our hood might not have been wise considering they never invited us to theirs."

The Six Mile kids stood in deep silence, and for good reasons. Rick felt he had been betrayed by the Sevens, mainly because no one from the Seven Mile Gang came to visit him in the hospital.

Meanwhile, Uddia and Niddy and other PAs were crewed up with some of the FAs. The two gangs were plotting together as one group for the first time in street history. I had given Niddy a twelve-pack of beer; I thought it was the least I could do since I wasn't going to be part of this year's Devil's Night event. The two gangs waited for Robin and some other members. Robin was an original PA; he was just as much of a leader in Mumford as Niddy and Uddia were. He was very vocal and would fight anytime, anywhere. While the two groups waited, they congregated on the corner like they were at a family reunion. They were all trying to get to know each other by firing up joints and smoking with a member from the other gang. Black Frost and Niddy were slowly becoming close friends. But tonight's plans were drastic; the two gangs planned to strike every Rich Boy hood this year, starting with Eight Mile Road.

When Robin and Wee arrived, all the kids from Puritan greeted them by loudly chanting, "PA down!" After a few more members arrived, they all formed a circle in the middle of the street. "Everybody ready?" Niddy said, walking to the middle of the circle. "Remember step one of our plan: we're going to steal fifteen cars from across Six Mile and meet up at that lot across Eight Mile Road and make our way back."

While the two urban gangs plotted against their rivals, Black Mike and ten cars full of Sevens from Mumford were rolling, heading straight to Six Mile. They had big plans of their own.

"This is what we going to do," Black Mike said in the lead car. "We're going to hit every Six Mile member house we know with spray paint, knock a few windows out, and head back to the hood." When they finally made it to Six Mile, the cars split up and rolled out toward different parts of the neighborhood. Black Mike, who was with Cowboy, P-Coal, and Jerry, drove straight over to Stan's house. They parked the car and headed out with guns and cans of spray paint. "Hey, I saw a fresh ass moped next door," Black Mike said. "I want it, so everyone be quiet." He violently shook a can of spray paint and then painted "Seven Mile" on Stan's front door. Romeo and a few other members were around the block doing the same to Bloka and Rick's house. The gang struck all around Rick's neighborhood, and residents were unaware what was happening.

After Romeo, Hash, and Lee finished spray painting Bloka's door, they headed to Six Mile Jim's house, which was next to Shell's house. Ironically, as they were walking to Jim's house, Niddy and a few PAs were coming down the same block. As Ant-Nice and Robin were complaining about swaying from the original plan, Z-ooh stopped by a tree and took a leak. They were the last of the two urban gangs left without a vehicle to head out to Eight Mile.

"Man, I just want to check on my woman's house before we do this," Niddy said with concern. "Especially since tonight is Devil's Night." As the four got closer, Niddy noticed Romeo and his two friends walking on Shell's lawn, and without hesitation he ran straight toward his girlfriend's house. He struck Romeo with an overhand right that sent the kid stumbling backward into a large bush. Romeo rolled off the bush and returned Niddy's punch with a big punch of his own. While the two squared off, Ant-Nice and Robin rushed to the scene and swung blow for blow with Lee and Hash. Unfortunately for Romeo, the close fight was turning out to be a one-sided debacle as the much slimmer and faster Niddy kept Romeo on his heels with a sequence of combinations. The punches blinded him as both his eyelids swelled up.

Z-ooh ran to the scene like a rhino and speared Romeo in the back with his large head. Suddenly a grey car full of Seven Mile BKs arrived in front of the house. But before they left their vehicle, loud gunshots sent everyone to the ground. When Niddy looked up, he couldn't believe what he saw. It was Wee and his boys, blasting pistols out of another car. "Run to the ride while we blast at them fools," he said, firing at the grey car. The shots shattered all the windows, causing the Seven Mile kids to jump out of the car like they were bailing out of an airplane. Two of the kids immediately started blasting back at Wee's car. When Wee ducked and fired back, Roni jumped out of the car and joined his friends on the ground. After a few minutes, though, all the shooters ran out of bullets, and loud clicking noises could easily be heard after the evil silence. Everyone who hit the ground hopped up and started fighting like a bunch of wild animals.

Niddy and the other PAs had to fight like hell if they wanted to get to Wee's car. It was twelve against seven. Wee reloaded his gun and started shooting again, surprising everybody except Roni, who had seen Wee reloading. He used that knowledge to his advantage by swinging his iron fist at his enemies just when Wee started shooting again. He led a pathway back to Wee's car by knocking out two kids along the way. Niddy and the others followed the pathway back to Wee's car and jammed into it like sardines.

"Let's get the hell out of here!" Niddy yelled as another car appeared and rammed into their vehicle. It was Black Mike and his boys, arriving on the scene like the cavalry.

Wee quickly started the car, backed up, and pulled away just as Black Mike and his boys got out of the car. As Wee drove away, Black Mike and company unloaded their guns on them. They angrily blasted at the car, causing everyone in the fleeing car to duck down nervously. Niddy and the PAs all rode with their heads down as the rain of bullets stormed on their vehicle. The shooting finally stopped when they reached the end of the block.

"Damn, talk about dodging a bullet," said Roni, after looking out the shot-out window. Everyone looked up and broke into laughter.

"Shit!" Black Mike cursed, as he heard the approaching sirens. It was a sound Black Mike was getting way too familiar with, a sound that had him running away once more.

Elsewhere at a deserted high school near Eight Mile, the Sconies and the Smurfs were partying like never before. Hundreds of them had gathered at the school's playground. "Eight o'clock, eight o'clock," they chanted. The chants echoed through the whole schoolyard as more and more members arrived. The Eight Mile Gangs were a big organization, more than a mere street gang. All their big fights were usually preplanned and thought out, but their easy access to money and guns made them even more dangerous. The gathering was planned by Bam-Bam, Danny, and a few old-school Eights. They were beyond the stupid pranks other gangs did on Devil's Night. The only thing they had planned on this night was to drink and mess with the many girls who came to the playground.

Meanwhile, Niddy and the carload of PAs pulled into the meet-up spot, an abandoned lot next to a bowling alley. The Puritan and Fenkle kids were already there, waiting impatiently for them to arrive. The two gangs had managed to boost nine cars from the Six Mile neighborhood. Some of the kids could steal a car as fast as eight seconds flat, and they made wagers on who could steal one the fastest.

Everyone got out of the car; they couldn't believe what they were seeing as they marveled at the nine stolen cars. Each one of the cars was brand-new or just a year or two old.

"What the fuck y'all do, rob a car lot?" Robin asked.

Their laughter echoed through the whole parking lot. Niddy and Black Frost got out and urged everyone to quiet down.

"All right, everybody calm down; it's time to get serious," Niddy ordered. "This is what we're going to do. We'll roll down the streets where some of the top Eights live at in nine different cars, and then we're going to dump everybody's trash out on their lawns. We are going to do that all the way to Seven Mile Road, then do the same to Seven Mile. After that, we dump all the stolen cars back across Six Mile and head back to the hood on foot."

Everyone then piled into the nine cars and left, leaving behind the bullet-riddled car Wee drove. Niddy's announcement had everyone hyped and ready for action. The two gangs were on a mission that night, a mission they planned to carry out to the fullest.

While they mobbed toward their mission, the Eights' gathering was being crashed by two patrol cars. The bright lights and sirens had everyone in the schoolyard running in panic. Some ran away on foot, while others piled in cars and forced their way out. The four policemen were shocked at the number of kids inside the schoolyard. The loud noise the kids made was what brought them to the scene. They had no idea there were that many kids inside until they entered the schoolyard. The officers were so surprised, they didn't even bother to detain anyone. They just called for backup and watched as the kids escaped. Bam-Bam and Danny had a preplanned escape route. Shane and Billy followed the two through a hole that led to Bam-Bam's black jeep. It was camouflaged under a tree outside the schoolyard fence. Three girls saw them going into the jeep and begged Billy for a ride, but the Smurf leader coldly turned them away. Shane knew one of the girls and wondered why Billy didn't let the girls in, but Bam-Bam knew all too well why the young Eight did what he did. One, the girls would have been a distraction; two, too many in the jeep would bring attention; and finally, the most important reason of all, they just weren't part of the plan.

Bam-Bam cautiously drove the jeep as kids invaded the streets like refugees. He looked out his window and smiled when he passed the fleeing kids. Even though the gathering had been cut short by the police, it gave him a thrill to know that he was part of assembling hundreds of members. He enjoyed the sense of power.

7

The last car load of kids was finishing their devilish prank of littering people's lawn with their own garbage. Inside the late-model car were Niddy, Roni, Ant-Nice, Black Frost, and Robin. They had six blocks to go to get to the new meet-up spot. Black Frost was driving and let them out of the car for the pranks. After that, he would pick them up at the end of that block. He did this repeatedly till they reached the last block to Seven Mile Road. The road was a borderline between the Seven and the Eight Mile Gangs. If you weren't driving or packing, it was unwise to cross that road.

"Hey Frost, we'll meet you at the meet-up spot on foot. It wouldn't make sense to pick us up at the corner, when the meet-up spot is across the street," said Niddy.

"All right, dog, but put some speed with that shit so we can get the hell out of here!" he replied, as he drove away slowly.

Roni started about four houses from the start of the block, while the others picked houses across the street. Roni had other things on his mind, besides just trashing people's front lawns. He wanted to steal a few things along the way. That was why the others went across the street. They did not want to be involved with stealing this night; everyone wanted to do pranks and go home. The others had seen him stealing on the other blocks and felt the stuff he was hauling was slowing them down. Roni knew what the others thought and why they chose the other side of the street. And usually he wouldn't have cared less about what they thought about him. But after flipping a few garbage cans, he noticed everyone was gone; he was the only one left out there. *Niddy and the others must be at the meet-up*, he thought.

All of a sudden, Roni could see his own shadow hover over him while he held the top of a garbage can. Then bright lights replaced his shadow; he was in a spotlight like he was a performer. Roni was so startled by the light, he dropped the garbage can lid and ran. Then a loud whistling sound came past his ear as gunshots rang out.

"Get that fool! Don't let him get away!" yelled Bam-Bam, as he drove wildly on the sidewalk. Billy hung out the back window with a three-eighty pistol, desperately shooting at Roni. But Roni moved with lightning speed as he zigzagged out of the way.

He ran into a backyard that was two houses from the corner of Seven Mile Road.

"Shit! He ran in that backyard; slow down!" Billy screamed after seeing Roni vanish into the dark. Bam-Bam continued to drive past the houses, figuring Roni would have to come out one of the yards to cross the dreaded road. But as soon as he turned the jeep back onto the road, they were right in front of the meet-up spot. Bam-Bam tried to stop and turn around, but it was too late. A barrage of bullets met them head-on. Roni, who was hiding in the backyard of the corner house, ran past the immobile jeep and quickly joined his friends across the street.

After stepping on the brakes, Bam-Bam ducked under the dashboard. He tried to put the jeep in park, but only managed to put it in neutral, as bullets tore through his hand. As the jeep slowly rolled down Seven Mile Road, screams could be heard from its floor. Hundreds of bullets tore through the jeep, causing it to rock sideways. When the shooting stopped, the jeep kept rolling until it crashed into a pole, ejecting Danny through the blown-out front windshield. The empty window frame he went through saved him from life-threatening injuries.

Danny grunted loudly when he hit the ground but was able to get up and walk to the heap of shot-up metal that once was called a jeep. The passenger door was so riddled with bullets, when he tried to open it, it fell off the hinges. The collapsed door surprised him so much he screamed and jumped back from the jeep. After taking a deep breath, he calmed down and looked in the jeep, gasping out loud when he noticed Bam-Bam slumped under the dashboard with glass stuck all over his back. When he pulled one piece out of his back, Bam-Bam yelled out loud from the pain. Danny quickly pulled him out of the jeep and laid him on the ground. He then went back to the jeep to check on Billy and Shane. When he opened the back door, a piece of Shane's bloody skull rolled onto his foot. He could see that Billy was dead from a gunshot wound. Shane was stuck in the smashed-up door on the other side of the jeep.

Danny tried to scream, but fluid replaced his screams and puke flowed out of his mouth instead. Even though he gagged aloud, he could hear the sounds of sirens. Danny knew he couldn't stay until the police came. So he decided to try and find all the guns in the jeep before they arrived. He turned Billy over and was shocked to see that he had died from his own gun.

Ten days after the horrors of Devil's Night, on Monday morning, as I joined my friends at the Dexter bus stop on Puritan Avenue, a car load of Eight Mile teenagers rode past us, hanging out the windows and yelling a very familiar slogan: "Eight o'clock!" My friends and I responded by chanting our own slogan—"PA down!"—as the car kept rolling. The Eight Mile Gang's chants could be heard a whole block away. Even when they were gone, the chants echoed in our heads.

"You see that shit, Niddy? Ever since Billy and Shane died in that car wreck, the Sconies and the Smurfs have been riding in our hood strong as hell," said Z-ooh.

"You right, but our hood is not the only one that's being patrolled. Word is they've been doing drive-bys all over the west side."

"Yeah," said Sid-Money. "I bet they were responsible for the drive-bys last week that left one of our homeys dead."

"It's possible," replied Niddy. "But we can't worry about something we really don't know."

"Well, I wish one of them dumb motherfuckers had gotten out, I would've blasted that fool all the way back to Eight Mile," said Sid-Money.

Everyone laughed as I pulled out a long joint to ease the moment. Niddy stared at his watch, figuring the bus should arrive in about ten minutes. He wondered if we had time to smoke it before the bus got there.

"Check this out, everybody," Niddy said as everyone gathered around the joint to keep the cold breeze from blowing it out. "This PA down shit has just jumped on another level. More and more kids are representing the hood in Mumford, even the Livernois PAs are getting deeper," he said proudly. "But we got to be careful or we could end up like our boy."

"Yeah, well, them Eights are two times deeper than us, dog," said Robin.

I took a couple of puffs off the joint and passed it to Robin, then stared at him oddly.

"Numbers ain't everything, Robin," I said. "What we have can rise above numbers any day, and that's heart. Most of them motherfuckers we be beefing with are hoes! Hell, some of them fools won't even fight unless they crewed up."

"He's right," Niddy replied. "All of them are Rich Boys that want to be gangsters. We are the real gangsters. We hustle for our loot on the streets, while they get theirs from momma!"

After Niddy's remarks, the loud brakes of the bus could be heard just a few blocks away.

"Ah shit, here come the bus," I said, putting the joint out on the side of the curb.

The screeching sounds from the bus replaced all of the talk and chatter, and the horrible fumes from the back engines killed the smell of the weed. When we got on the bus, we were so high off the reefer, we laughed all the way to the back of the bus. We playfully fought over the remaining hot seats; everyone got a seat except Sid-Money. Sitting in the back was common among kids in Detroit around this time. The hot seats in the back were like sitting in royalty when it was cold.

"What happen to Uddia?" I asked. "He took today off or something?"

"He got his car fix now," Niddy replied. "More than likely he had to take his brother to work, and I bet he went to school from there."

"That's right, I forgot Joe was working on his car, but what about school? Don't tell me he dropped out?" I asked.

"Naw, dog, but he did get kicked out of the whole Detroit public school system; he go to a school out in Southfield now."

"Good!"

I looked out the window and noticed our bus ride was almost over. I wished Uddia was with us for our morning journey, figuring we may need his help.

"Did anybody hear about the new club?" said Sid-Money. "They call it the Get Down Club; it's for kids that are fifteen to seventeen years old. It opens this weekend, and the building is big as hell!"

"Oh yeah? Where is it?" Niddy asked.

"On Puritan, God damn it!"

"No shit, a club in our hood?" Niddy replied, and then he pulled the bus cord. "Man, we about to run that bitch."

I daydreamed about the club as I got off the bus, and my thoughts continued to drift as I got closer to the school. The club, I thought, should bring something good to the hood, especially since the Puritan neighborhoods had no fun spots we could actually walk to. It was obvious the Rich Boy neighborhoods were treated better than the poor ones when it came down to the hangout spots. Rich Boy neighborhoods had recreation centers, skating rinks, and luxury stores, while Puritan was known for the Candy Store and an old skating rink that had been shut down for years. My thoughts vanished when I entered the school, and I immediately jumped into my ready-to-fight mode on the way to my locker. This was common among all the PAs who went to Mumford; we stayed keyed and ready for anything.

Elsewhere in Mumford, Black Mike, P-Coal, and Jerry were just arriving at their lockers on the second floor. Many members were already there, waiting to greet them with handshakes and high fives. The past few days, the Seven Mile kids had taken a lot of heat from the police. Even though Black Mike and his gang of Sevens weren't around when Bam-Bam's jeep was shot up, they were getting much of the blame. Roni had been spotted in the jeep that night near Seven Mile Road. Since no one in the jeep had seen their attackers, everyone assumed they were from Seven Mile. That being said, the Seven Mile Gang's individual beefs with Six Mile and the PAs were also in the open. Even though they had nothing to do with the death of the two Eight Mile kids, no gang was more delighted at the outcome than the Sevens. Black Mike knew all too well that Billy's wild leadership of the Smurfs would surely be missed. Although he never liked Billy, he had the utmost respect for the deceased young gangster. Black Mike and his friends felt this was a good time for the Sevens to get ultimate revenge against the Eights, especially since other top Eight Mile members like Bam-Bam and Frog were no longer attending Mumford. The rumor was that their parents had requested a transfer for their sons.

When Black Mike walked into French class with his cousin Lee, the first person he noticed was Niddy, who was writing on a sheet of paper. He glared at Niddy before he sat down, hoping to get some type of reaction. His mean stares went unnoticed, as Niddy ignored his entrance and continued writing. I, on the other hand, noticed it all. I smiled at Black Mike, rubbing the cold steel magnolia that sat snuggly in my school bag before taking out my pencil. Black Mike really wanted to engage in a fight with the PAs over the Devil's Night incident. His late arrival to the scene that night didn't sit well with him either. "Damn, got to stick with the plan," Black Mike said softly, remembering the agreement he and the other top Sevens made. The plan was to take out the headless Eight Mile Gang and ignore the uprising of the PAs.

Mrs. Jackson walked from her table to the front of the class. "All right, people," she said. "We have two new students in the class; their names are Rally and Matt. Would you two please stand up and introduce yourselves?"

After the two students introduced themselves and sat down, Mrs. Jackson passed out assignments for the class. The introduction seemed to ease the tension the class was feeling for a moment. Now, all attention was on the two new students. Matt had been appointed Mumford's new Six Mile leader by his peers, while Rally was the newest member of the PAs. Matt and Niddy had been childhood friends at Post Middle School. When he arrived at Mumford, his longtime friendship with Niddy instantly created peace between their gangs.

I had accepted Rally as a new PA member, but because of a recent fight, I didn't accept him as a friend. We had a disagreement in the candy store the previous week that had turned into a small fight. I had gotten the worse end of it and wanted revenge, but it never happened. Niddy and Uddia liked Rally, which basically kept down the drama. The two leaders broke up near fights between the two of us many times and had been trying to keep us in line ever since. Defeat in any form was something I thought was unacceptable. Especially since I had won close to fifty fights since I was eleven years old and had never lost before. Even though I didn't show it, I decided to bury the hatchet and let bygones be bygones.

While we did our French assignments, just down the hall, in the algebra classroom, Uddia, Ant-Nice, and Z-ooh were chilling out in the back of the class. Then suddenly, an Eight Mile Sconie named Key-Key started staring at Uddia. Uddia knew the Eights didn't like him, especially after the beatdown he gave Frog. Ant-Nice and Z-ooh looked at Uddia and knew off the top he wasn't going to tolerate the staring.

"Hey bitch," Uddia yelled across the room. "You got a problem or something?"

Key-Key's only response was the familiar Eight Mile slogan. "Eight o'clock!" he yelled as Mr. Keith, the teacher, got out of his chair. Uddia knew all too well why Key-Key had done that; it was to get the attention of his friends in the class.

What a hoe! This motherfucker stares me down for about ten minutes then looks for help when I don't back down, Uddia thought as he left his table and walked toward Key-Key without a second thought. Mr. Keith yelled at Uddia to sit down, but he kept going. When he arrived at Key-Key's table, he stood over the kid like a giant over a fly. His size differential was so astronomical it seemed unfair.

"Yeah, I don't give a fuck about your boys," Uddia said, standing over Key-Key with clenched fists. "So what up now, bitch? What up now?" Uddia screamed, and then he viciously slapped Key-Key out of his chair like he was a rag doll. The slap was so loud that students in the hallway heard it, and they were more than twenty-five feet away.

Ant-Nice couldn't believe what he was seeing, as he and other PAs rose out of their chairs after noticing the Eights doing the same. Fortunately, before the two gangs left their tables, Mr. Keith came in between Uddia and the fallen Key-Key and told everyone else to sit down.

"Everybody calm down and sit back down in your seat or get a first-class ticket to the principal's office," he said.

After Mr. Keith's comment, all the students backed off and sat back down. The teacher then picked Key-Key up from the floor and told the bloody-nosed student to go to the office and explain to the principal what happened. After he left, Mr. Keith looked out his classroom, hoping to see a truant officer, but he could not find one. So he decided to take Uddia to the office himself. "Let's go, Uddia," he ordered, leading him out of the class with his arm firmly around his shoulder.

"Well Uddia, it looks like you really did it this time," said Mr. Keith, still holding him by the shoulder. "You knew you only had one more chance; now it looks like your time is up."

"You right, my time is up," Uddia replied. "So it doesn't make sense that I go to the office already knowing the outcome!"

Uddia then yanked his shoulder away and stormed out of the building, leaving Mr. Keith standing speechless in the hallway. Uddia walked into the parking lot; he had known that this day was coming. When he made it to his car, he pulled half a joint out of the ashtray and lit it. He stared at the school for a moment, with one leg hanging out of the car, and hit the weed a few times before starting the car, and then he peeled out of the parking lot like he was on a raceway. When he reached the traffic light on Wyoming Road, he heard the loud school bell ringing. He looked over at the school one last time.

Hours after Uddia's departure, the school was like an accident waiting to happen as students filled the hallways when the bell rang. It didn't take long for the whole school to know about the dramatic slap Uddia had given Key-Key. Many students thought violence was surely going to occur afterward, but it never happened. The Eights were in no position to lose any more members in the school, especially since they had lost all their top leaders in the past month. Bam-Bam, Frog, Shane, and Billy were no longer there to lead them in battle.

The Six Mile Gang was on the first floor, dealing with a dilemma of they own. The truce they had with the Seven Mile Gang was now officially broken, and they were discussing plans to attack them.

Elsewhere in the school, most of the Sevens were just leaving their lockers and going to their sixth hour class.

The PAs, whose lockers were on the same floor, were also headed to their last class. Unfortunately, Niddy and I had to travel alone to our last class. But that was the least of our problems. My sixth hour class was football, and Niddy's was weightlifting. The gymnasium was right next to the Seven Mile lockers. We had to walk past the lockers every day to get to class. The only other way was going downstairs to the first floor, beneath the entrance. Niddy and I never wanted to go that way, which would make us late. The main reason, however, was that going the other way would make us look like cowards, something neither one of us wanted.

Fortunately, today the Seven Mile hallway was empty when we arrived at the class double doors. After we entered the gym, we split up and headed to our classes.

Niddy and I dreamed of one day being on the football team, and we felt these classes would help fulfill those dreams. The dreams seemed to drift further and further away, though, as our wild activities affected our attendance and grades. We needed at least a C+ average to even be considered for the tryouts. It was a requirement the coaches and teachers always stressed. Since I was the brightest member in the group when it came down to the books, the bad grades seemed to affect me more than anyone. I knew without a doubt that I could do better if I wasn't part of a gang.

As class proceeded, I started daydreaming about school and my gang obligations. After giving it much thought, I came to the chilling conclusion that in order for me to graduate from Mumford someday, I would have to stop the gang banging. The only problem was, in order for me to do that, I would have to drop out of the PAs, something I was not prepared to do.

Sixth hour finally ended with no violence, which was still highly anticipated after Uddia and Key-Key's altercation.

While most kids celebrated the joy of leaving school, Ant-Nice and I were getting ready for one more class, seventh hour. The two of us kicked it with Niddy and the others at the lockers before mobbing to class. The PA Gang left the school fifty members deep, basically daring anyone to fuck with them. They walked grimly past every major gang in the school before reaching the Dexter bus stop on Curtis Road. Seconds later, two buses arrived in front of the mob of kids, and they all tried to jam in them, fearing there wouldn't be enough seats. Their fears were correct, as Niddy and Rally were left off the bus because of no room. The two PAs waited for the next bus and felt relieved when they spotted one coming just three lights away. While they waited for the bus, Rally, who knew I still didn't like him, felt this was the time to express himself.

"Hey Niddy, tell your boy Muscles I want to be friends, not enemies."

"He'll come around, dog," replied Niddy. "Just give him time, you'll find out he's one of the coolest guys to know."

Suddenly, Niddy and Rally stopped talking and shifted their attention to a slow-moving vehicle they spotted coming behind them from the school. The mysterious car suddenly stopped about fifteen feet away from Niddy and Rally, and four kids hopped out of the car, waving pistols, and came toward the bus stop, chanting, "Eight o'clock," at the top of their lungs.

Rally and Niddy both pulled out large pistols with unapproachable speed and fired at the four kids without hesitation. The gunshots took the four kids clearly by surprise, as they all ducked and retreated back to their vehicle. Ironically, the bus arrived at the same time the shooting started, and the driver panicked and froze at the wheel. The two PAs quickly ran onto the waiting bus and were greeted with screams from the passengers as smoke seeped from their pistols. Niddy stared at the bus driver hard and knew he was scared as hell. The driver looked petrified, so Niddy wanted to ease his mind a little.

"Just do your job and drive this motherfucker," he said. "And you won't have a problem with us, dog."

The relieved driver pulled away from the bus stop.

Meanwhile back at Mumford, thirty minutes had elapsed, and everyone was impatiently waiting for the seventh hour to end. There were still ten classes in progress, and there were at least four Seven Mile members in each class. This was a high percentage, considering there was an average of twelve students in each one of the classes. Seventh hour in many students' eyes was obviously the hour of the Sevens. Ever since their big fight with the Eights early this year, they numbers in Mumford had been growing drastically, especially seventh hour.

Black Mike, who also had a seventh hour class, felt this was the best hour to kick some shit off. He knew the Eights' attention now was focused more on the PAs, especially after Uddia's slap and departure. The word around the school was that Key-Key was still in the office. The battered student was still awaiting his father's arrival, which gave Black Mike an idea. The Seven Mile leader raised his hand in the classroom and asked to use the restroom. Once he was in the hallway, he went to three other classes and pointed out each member from the doorway. The pointing gesture was a secret signal the Sevens used when they wanted to get a member out of class. P-Coal, Jerry, and Calley left their classes and met up with Black Mike on the second floor near the principal's office.

"Calley," Black Mike said, with his arm around his shoulder, "I want you to go in the office and hit that kid Key-Key in the mouth, and run out of there as fast as you can."

Calley, who was far from being an aggressive soldier, was caught clearly off guard by Black Mike's orders. The look on his face showed he had no intention of going into the office. "Man, I'm sorry, dog, I can't do that," he said.

Black Mike then removed his arm from Calley's shoulder like he was touching something poisonous. Before Black Mike could say anything, Jerry walked straight toward the office. All eyes now were on Jerry; everyone stopped talking and watched him go into the office with no hesitation.

Key-Key's first reaction when he saw Jerry enter the office was to defend himself. But when Jerry walked past him and went to the office counter, Key-Key relaxed. That was a grave mistake, as Jerry turned, picked up a wooden chair, and ran at him. Key-Key raised his arm, attempting to block the chair, but Jerry smashed it over his arm. The chair broke into many pieces over his body. The impact was so violent, it knocked him out and broke five bones in his arms and face. After the brutal assault, the school clerks screamed, which sent Jerry running out of the office. Black Mike and the others saw the whole thing and directed him out of the school.

After Jerry left, Black Mike noticed there were only fifteen minutes left till the final bell rang. Realizing that, he knew it would be a waste of time to go back to class, so he headed out of the dreaded school.

8

our days passed by, and the November weather was getting colder as light snow fell on Detroit. That Friday afternoon, I got off the bus after my school day was over and headed home. I ran through an alley straight to my house. When I closed the door behind me, I waved to my moms and trotted up the spiral stairs that led to my room. I closed the door of my room like I had a pot of gold in there. I took my coat off and safely removed the pistol I had borrowed. I unloaded it, slid it under the bed, and then grabbed a twenty bag of reefer from my hiding spot and stuffed it in my pocket.

"Yeah, tonight's the night," I said, pulling my best pair of long-pocket Levis out my closet and pressing them with an iron. The oversize pants were the new style in Detroit. Everyone made sure their pants were one size bigger than normal. I was ready for a big night. First I was meeting up with my cousin Moe to discuss the present beef between the Eights and the PA Gang. I also had plans to meet up with Niddy and the other members at the candy store before we headed to the grand opening of the Get Down Club. It was about four o'clock, and the club opened at nine. I knew I had to get a move on if I was going to complete this mission.

While I got ready, I couldn't shake the thought that Roni, my main boy from the hood, couldn't get into the club because of his age. He was fourteen, and the age limit was fifteen to seventeen years old. The word around the school was security was going to be at an all-time high, and they were going to use metal detectors at the doors. I called Roni to see if he wanted to mob with me to Moe's house. I felt that was the least I could do since he couldn't go to the club like everyone else.

"Hello, hey what's up, Roni? You want to go with me to my cousin's house across Eight Mile Road?"

"Eight Mile! Are you crazy, man? You must have forgotten that we're beefing strong with them fools."

"Don't worry; Moe's a top member from Eight Mile Road, and I got the green light to his house. I am not to be touched."

"Well, dig that; if it's like that, I'll meet you at your house in a minute."

After I hung up, I decided to give Mia a call. I had talked to her every night and was really enjoying her conversations. She was highly intelligent, but far from a nerd. She was just as fine as any fine girl in the school and sweeter than the meaning of sweetness. I definitely liked her and planned to hook up with her very soon.

Not too far away from my house near Six Mile Road, Bloka, Matt, and twelve others were crewed up on bikes in front of a record store. They anxiously waited in the cold for Bloka's command. "Let's roll!" Bloka ordered, leading the way down Six Mile Road like a sheriff and his posse. When they reached a traffic light and rode past the cars waiting at the light, the sound of doors locking could be heard. One woman was so scared that she ran a red light as soon as she noticed the group of kids. "Damn! Well, I guess you can't blame her," Bloka said, laughing out loud.

As they rode, Bloka's mind cleared and he started thinking about their destination: the field at Mumford. All week long, rumors spread that the Seven Mile Gang was going to have a football game amongst themselves on the field. And all week long, the Six Mile Gang had planned to take clean advantage of it and make the Sevens pay for their Devil's Night treachery. About twenty more members were supposed to meet Bloka at the school, and ten more from the hood were coming later. Even though they were very prepared, he still wondered if they had enough members to fight.

Matt looked at his watch and figured they would reach Mumford in about ten minutes. Matt always kept a pistol with him, but he and a few others were the only ones packing for this occasion. And it wasn't because they couldn't bring more hardware; it was because they knew they were already targets for the police. Bloka didn't like guns, especially since his good friend Rick was in the hospital because of one. He loved to fight and looked forward to cracking some heads on Mumford field.

"Hey, Bloka, let's stop at a store and get some goodies before we make it to the school," Matt suggested.

"Damn, dog, your ass is always hungry, don't you eat at home, motherfucker?" replied Bloka, bringing laughter from the others. Nonetheless, they all stopped at the nearest store and went in.

Roni and I were just boarding the Greenfield to Eight Mile bus with transfer slips. We were dressed to kill wearing Army coats and hiking boots that went well with our sagging long-pocket Levis. Everyone on the bus watched as we walked to the back of the bus, but more attention was on the way Roni walked. He was cocky with exceptionally big arms for his age, causing him to look very intimidating. After getting comfortable in the hot seats at the back of the bus, my mind started to drift back to the first bus Roni and I had boarded. I had seen Bloka and his crew out the window and said, "Look at them fools riding bicycles in the snow. They got to be up to no good." I never liked riding buses and wouldn't be riding one today if the mission wasn't so important. I reflected on Moe's reaction when I had told him the PA Gang and the Eight Mile Gang were feuding in Mumford. I knew that it really was bothering him; that day on the phone, he said, "We need to talk about this shit."

Before my mind drifted any further, I felt a hard tap on my shoulder and then jumped out of my seat like I was waking up out of a dream. "This is where we get off at, ain't it?" Roni said playfully, and then he pulled the bus cord.

While we proceeded with our mission, Bloka and thirty-five Sixes were storming the field at Mumford like unchained barbarians. Black Mike, Cowboy, P-Coal, and other Seven Mile members were on the field. The Six Mile Gang had to run about fifty yards to reach them, which gave the Sevens ample time to brace themselves for the attack. Bloka was the first to make contact by exploding through the Sevens' front, like a running back crashing through a hole. He took a few kids out of the fight with the move and continued to swing with no mercy.

"Six minutes," Matt chanted, after busting a Seven Mile member in the mouth who was coming behind Bloka. The field looked like a true battlefield. The two gangs fought each other to a standstill for ten minutes straight. Unfortunately, the football game the Seven Mile Gang had played earlier was starting to tire them, as their swings felt like a thousand bricks were holding them down. The close fight quickly turned into a slaughter, as members from Seven Mile Road started falling. Black Mike and the Sevens continued to fight, displaying the type of heart you only saw in the movies, but heart alone wasn't going to win this fight.

Meanwhile, Roni and I were just a block away from Moe's house, walking down Eight Mile Road. Roni's distinctive walk was bringing us unwanted attention. Gang members at the corner stared at us coldly and then started yelling, "Eight o'clock," at the top of their lungs when we walked by. My first thought was to whip out the large pistol from under my coat and start blasting at the fools. But then I remembered the green light Moe had given me through the hood and decided not to make a move unless Moe's promise was broken. Roni had turned around and taunted the Eights with his pistol; he had no problem letting the bangers know that he was packing.

After passing the Eight Mile Gang without altercation, Roni said, "I knew them motherfuckers was some hoes; they didn't do shit!"

"That's where you're wrong at, Roni," I replied. "You must have forgotten about the green light my cousin gave us to mob through this hood. Those soldiers on the corner were more than likely ordered not to do anything unless we did something."

When we got to Moe's house, we walked onto the porch, and Moe opened the door.

"What up, cuz? You're late," Moe said, eyeing his watch. "I was starting to worry about you; come in." He led us through the living room straight to the back door, and the first thing I noticed was Clyde and Bam-Bam. Without thinking, I pulled my pistol from up under my coat with the intent to shoot the gang leader. Roni also pulled his gun out, but Moe intervened before matters really got out of hand.

"Put them guns away, respect my house," Moe said, with obvious anger. "Put them away now!"

I gave Moe a funny look but immediately put my hardware away and motioned Roni to do the same.

"What's up with this shit, man? You told me it was just going to be me and you," I said.

"You right, I did, so why did you bring Roni then?"

"Man, you know Roni's my boy; besides, if I knew it was a problem, I would've never brought him."

"I'm not tripping on that, dog, just like you shouldn't trip on the guests in my house!"

"All right, Moe, I get your point, and I'm sorry for the gun show; it won't happen again. Let's move on and get to the reason why I'm here."

After everyone shook hands and ended the altercation, Moe led us into his garage, where he took his friends when company came over. Moe motioned us to sit down and began to speak.

"All right, Bam-Bam, let's start with you. Why do you think the PA Gang can't get along with us, dog?" he asked.

"Uddia started all this shit, Moe," he said, staring at Roni. "Ever since he snuck my boy Frog in the hallway, tension has grown between us."

"Well, personally," I said, glaring at Bam-Bam, "I got no problem with no one unless you fuck with me, my family, or my homeboys. And Uddia's my boy. If I recall, Bam-Bam, you weren't there at the fight but I was, and I'm here to tell you your boy Frog pushed that fight to the fullest; believe me, nobody got snuck; that's my word!"

Clyde then rose up out of his chair with eyes that glistened so much it looked like he had been crying.

"What about Billy?" he shouted. "Rumors say the PAs were behind the shooting that left my boy dead!"

"Yeah, well I heard those same rumors," I retorted. "And that's all they are, rumors. The fact is Billy died from his own gun, not a PA's."

Clyde's glistening eyes went blank; he knew there was no proof to the rumors. Bam-Bam, on the other hand, stared at Roni during the whole conversation, trying to make out where he had seen him before. Roni, who never knew who had fired the guns at him out of the jeep that dreadful night before Halloween, would more than likely shit a brick if he knew that he was sitting right across from him now.

"All right, I think everybody has said enough; listen up," said Moe. "I got a real solution to this problem. Clyde, you're going to run the Smurfs in Mumford with no problem from the PAs, because far as I'm concerned, our beef with them is over. Now, let's smoke this Afghan weed and make peace like the Indians!" Laughter followed, easing the obvious tension everyone was feeling. Before Moe fired up the joint, I pulled him to the side and asked him a question that had been on my mind for a long time.

"Hey cuz, I want you to look me in the eye and tell me what you did with that Uzi that night."

He looked straight in my eyes and said, "You know I don't talk my business, but I'm going to make an exception this time. I sold it. I needed the money more than I needed the hardware, plus I had heard about your recent beefs and didn't want to see you catch a case with my killing machine."

"So you had nothing to do with that drive-by at that party on Six Mile Road?" I questioned.

"Hell, no. You know I'm not down with no cowardly ass shit like that," he responded harshly.

"Sorry, cuz, I'm not trying to sound like a cop, but the word in the street was the gunman at the party had an Uzi, and I prayed you weren't involved!"

"Well, you could stop worrying because you can best believe I am not the only nigga in Detroit with an Uzi. Besides, my Uzi was a baby, remember? The papers said the killing machine that smoked those kids at the party was a large Uzi."

Those words were like beautiful music to my ears. Although my cousin was crazy in the streets, I knew deep down inside he wasn't down with that type of violence.

Meanwhile, bloody and injured kids lay all over Mumford field. Most of them were Seven Mile members, but a good number of Six Mile LAs were also injured. The fight was still going on, despite the faint sounds of approaching sirens. When the police finally arrived, everyone stopped fighting and ran off the bloodstained field, scattering like a flock of birds. Black Mike was the first one out; he jumped over two squad cars that barricaded the nearest exit. Everyone else found their own means of escape, leaving the fallen and injured at the mercy of the police.

When Officers Jones and Brooks stepped out of the squad car, they couldn't believe what they saw. The field of injured kids was so disturbing to see, a rookie policeman ran back to his squad car and threw up.

"The Romans couldn't have done worse," said Officer Brooks.

"Yeah, right, it look like someone threw them at the lions," replied Officer Jones as the two walked through the injured kids on the field.

"This gang shit is really getting out of hand, Jones; if we don't do something about it soon, we're going to see far worse than this!"

"I agree, Brooks, but the amazing thing about this shit is most of these kids on the ground are middle class students."

"Yeah, Rich Boys compared to the kids in the ghetto; they come from a good upbringing and still do this dumb shit," Brooks replied while helping an injured kid up from the ground.

"That go to show you, it's not all about where you live, it's how you live," Jones said, counting how many kids were injured on the field. "Twenty," he said, under his breath. The horrific sight was so vulgar that it left a sour taste in his mouth.

Ten miles away and two hours later, Roni and I were just meeting up with the boys at the Candy Store. I had already filled Niddy in about the peace treaty on Moe's phone before we arrived.

"About time you two made it; we were starting to wonder if those Eights had got in that ass," said Niddy.

Almost every PA in the Candy Store was ready for the grand opening of the Get Down Club. Everyone from across Puritan Avenue wanted to be there because it was located on Puritan. The word in the street was many older girls, some as old as nineteen, were also coming for the event. Some of the older guys made plans to hang out in their cars near the club just to holler at the pretty girls who came in and out.

After kicking the shit for fifteen minutes, the PAs left the candy store and headed to the new club on foot. Roni tagged along, knowing he couldn't get in, but he decided to try anyway with his older brother Bryant's license. The glow on everybody's face was enough for him to at least try.

"Hey cuz, you think they going to let you in?" Niddy asked.

"I don't know," Roni replied. "But I'm going to try anyway; I got Bryant's ID, and I took a big risk getting it, so I'm going to at least try and get some fun out of this shit."

Niddy hoped he would be able to get in, but he knew Roni didn't look much like Bryant, so he didn't think his plan would work.

Twenty-five to thirty PA gang members mobbed their way toward the club with pure excitement, all figuring to have the best time of their lives. As we got closer, Travis rolled up some of his Afghan weed and handed it to me with some matches, instructing me to share it with Roni.

"That's that good shit," he said. "Since you two missed out earlier, smoke that to yourselves."

Travis was a well-known PA who loved guns, like his older brother Boone. He was a likable person but was very dangerous when he was high. On one occasion, he came very close to shooting Roni and me by mistake, all because he was high. Ever since then, he was known as "Happy," as in "trigger-happy."

After ten minutes of walking, we finally got to the club. It was a little after eight thirty and outside, the club was already packed.

"Damn, dog," said Niddy. "I see about a hundred girls in that line; hell, it can't be no more than a hundred and fifty people in the whole line."

"That means it's more girls than hard-heads, which means no one should have a problem with getting they own squeeze," said Uddia.

"Man, look at how those girls look; most these bitches are from different hoods, dog. I never seen some of these girls before," Ant-Nice said.

The line shifted forward, as the doors opened and kids entered the club. All the PAs, including the Livernois group, who just arrived on the scene, stormed the line as it continued to shift forward.

"Man," Robin said, "I bet that most of the hard-heads here are from Puritan."

"You may be right, Robin," Niddy replied. "But what do you expect? It's not too many fools alive that would even walk in our hood, let alone come to a club here."

"True, but it wouldn't matter how many would come; this is our hood: we run this shit!" Robin said proudly.

Even though the PA Gang seemed to have overwhelming odds going into the club, Roni and I still felt funny being in line without our pistols. We had left them at my house before we went to the Candy Store, figuring that because the club was close by our friend Wee's house, we could run there for weapons if we needed to.

Roni, who was getting caught up in the pretty girls and the bright lights, was in for a big disappointment.

"Sorry, kid, this is not your ID, you're not old enough!" said the armed doorman. Roni was so embarrassed by the rejection that he thought of picking up a brick and hitting the guard. He wisely decided not to because of his friends, figuring it would spoil our fun. After he departed, the teenagers continued to pack into the club like sardines. The building's capacity was three hundred people, but because this was the only club for youths on the west side of Detroit, the owners expected more. Once all the PAs were inside, all the hanging around bullshit went out the window. We split up and browsed through the packed building, hyped and ready for fun. Niddy, Uddia, and I stayed pretty close, figuring some fool might be stupid enough to start trouble.

The first thing I noticed when I went in was a large poster that read, "When you leave this building, there are no readmissions."

"Hey Uddia, I guess that sign is to keep down all the back and forth shit, you know, like, once you in, you in," I said.

"Yeah, well, I think they don't want motherfuckers running out to their cars and coming back in with weapons," Uddia replied.

"Hey Uddia," said Niddy, interrupting our conversation. "Let's go to the bathroom and drink some of this yak I got before this shit really pops off. Since you don't drink,

Muscles, you might as well hold it down till we come out, it won't be ten minutes."

"All right, dog, I'll wait," I replied, "but not right here. I'm going to find somewhere to sit till you two come out."

After Uddia and Niddy departed, I went to the refreshment bar and sat in the lounge area. It was just a few yards from where we had been standing, and it was a perfect place to sit and see my friends come out of the bathroom. The dance floor was packed with girls doing all the latest dance steps, while the young gangsters jocked them like fresh meat. *Damn, too bad my boy couldn't get in*, I thought, thinking about Roni.

Suddenly, that thought disappeared when I noticed a young guard staring at me from across the lounge. The stare turned into a glare as we both made direct eye contact with each other. The staring scene went on for a few minutes before we both left our seats and walked furiously toward each other. Everyone looked on as we came toward each other with determination and balled fists. However, as we got near each other, the great Uddia appeared and jumped in between us.

"I'm not going to let you two fight," he said, "because both of you are my friends. Besides, tonight's the night to have fun."

Uddia kept his large body in between us. My mind was still set on fighting, but at the same time I knew my good friend was right, so I let it go.

"You right, Uddia, it's way too many females in here to fuck with than to trip on this weak shit," I replied, and then I reached out for a handshake. "No harm did, dog, no harm done."

After the two of us reconciled, Uddia and I walked over to the dance floor and stood next to Buddy and Sid-Money. Buddy was a PA who went to Central High, a Linwood-dominated school. He was a loner at the school and spent most of his time chasing pretty girls.

"Hey Buddy," I said, after noticing a fine girl across the dance floor checking me out. "That girl over there has been staring at me ever since I came in the building. I would have made a move on her, but I seen you two hugging in the line, figuring she was your woman or something."

"I'm always hugging women, dog; I'm a player, remember? I don't care about bitches like that; the girl is in my class, and she was just giving me a hug. If you want to holler at her, don't let that stop you; handle your business."

"Muscles not about to holler at that, Buddy, he's too God damn shy," Niddy said as he arrived on the tail end of the conversation.

"Fuck you, Niddy," I joked. "I holler when I want to holler, not when someone else want me to holler. Besides, while we're talking shit, I just watched her turn three people down, and all of them were young ballers."

Buddy placed his hand on my shoulder and said, "Just because she didn't dance with them doesn't mean she won't give you a play. If she's been giving you the eye like you said, then she might be waiting for you to ask her to dance."

After he said that, I went over and approached the fine girl with no hesitation and asked her for a dance. She was a light-skinned knockout who demanded attention, and she had pretty eyes to go along with her smile. She said, "Yes, I'll dance with you."

Everyone, including my friends, gasped when the two of us hit the dance floor, but no one was more surprised than me. I danced close to her, doing the popular dance called the German Smurf. She responded by turning around and bouncing her ass on me like it was a privilege. I then grabbed her small waist from behind and started doing the freaky dance. Onlookers stared at us like they were watching *Soul*

Train as I got harder and harder from her bouncing ass. The closer I danced to her, the more she bounced her ass on me. I was obviously embarrassed but continued to do the freaky dance with her.

Damn, I know she feel me, she got to, I said to myself, while beads of sweat started coming down my face.

We "freaked" through three songs before the DJ finally took a five-minute break. The girl smiled at me and then left the dance floor like she was never there. I followed her and asked her for her name.

"Eva," she said.

"I'm sorry," I said, nudging my head close to her. "I don't think I heard you right from all the noise in here; did you say evil or Eva?"

"Eva, boy, I'm not evil, I'm a nice person."

"My name is James; I'm sorry, I wasn't trying to call you evil."

"It's okay."

"So, Eva, do you have a boyfriend?"

"No, do you have a girlfriend?"

"Nope, but I need one; what's up, you going to help me out, baby?"

Eva looked directly into my eyes and smiled, not bothering to answer the question, but the look in her eyes made me think of the possibilities. Suddenly, two pretty boys stepped to Eva with freaky dancing on their minds, but she turned them both down cold. After the cold diss, Buddy, who had been watching us since we hit the dance floor, approached her also.

"Hey Eva," he said. "I never saw you dance like that before! Can your boy get a dance in too?"

"I'm sorry, Buddy, but I'm dancing with James again," she said, pulling me by the hand when the music started playing again.

I was surprised but joined her on the floor once more. While we were having a good time, Niddy and the other PAs were having the time of their lives in a different manner. They danced wildly to the music like they owned the dance floor. We were easily the largest gang in the building. Uddia and Ant-Nice were the first to chant our gang's name on the floor, and it created a chain reaction inside the place that seemed to shake the whole building. The chanting went in sequence with the music, as if it was a part of the song. Even the kids who weren't part of the PAs chanted the gang's name, so they wouldn't be cited as outsiders.

An hour passed by, and tension floated in the air as the chanting in the club started to get wild. Security tried to stop the chanting by yelling at the teenagers to stop, but they were largely ignored. As they continued to chant, Eva, who was still dancing with me, looked worried. She stopped dancing and embraced me with a tight grip, a grip that revealed the fear in her body. After feeling her vibe, I quickly led her off the dance floor to the refreshment area. I ordered two ginger ales and held her hand till we sat down at a table.

"Those PA boys are about to start fighting, aren't they?" she asked, trying to regain her composure.

"Nope, I doubt it, they just hyped up a little, but they won't start nothing with nobody unless you start it with them first," I replied.

"Oh really," she said, with sarcasm ringing in her voice. "It seems to me you know a lot about those boys; are you a PA, James?"

"If I tell you, will it make a difference in me getting your number?" I replied.

"Only if you lie to me," she retorted.

"All right, yeah, I'm down with the PAs, I'm down with them till the day I die," I said proudly.

"I would have never guessed," she said with a surprised tone in her voice. "You just don't seem like the type to be involved with gangs."

"What, you think I'm a square or something?"

"No, that's not what I mean, it's the way you carry yourself. It's like you got this focus thing going on with you, like you know what you want in life."

"You're right, Eva, and you is what I want."

Eva revealed a smile that would've made the meanest man in the world happy; she had that type of glow around her. We partied through the night till the club finally closed.

9

Three weeks passed, and by early December, Mumford was back to normal. Students were back in school after the ten-day Thanksgiving break. The kids who had been injured in the schoolyard debacle were also back in school.

Black Mike and P-Coal were headed to fifth hour, while Romeo and other Seven Mile members were posted up at their lockers. Niddy and I were coming from the opposite direction. Usually, the hallways were cleared out by this time of the day when we went to our gym class. Today was different, though, as a number of Seven Mile members lingered in the halls. Gym class had recently been changed from sixth hour to fifth hour, to calm the violence that always seemed to come at the end of that hour. Romeo, who didn't like Niddy, stood by his locker with his arms folded while Niddy and I walked past him.

"Hey Niddy," Romeo yelled out when we walked by. "What up now, dog? What you want to do?"

"It's whatever you want to do, dog, whatever you want to do," Niddy replied, after stopping dead in his tracks.

Six of Romeo's friends came from their lockers with short bats and brass knuckles and tried to surround Niddy, but they ignored me. *Damn, they ignoring the hell out of me, must think I won't get down or something*, I thought to myself, and then I jumped in between Niddy and the crowd of kids. I put my hand in my bag and cocked the hammer back on my gun; at the loud click, every kid in the hallway stepped back. I never pulled the gun out of the bag, though; I just held the bag with one hand and kept my finger on the trigger of the gun with the other. I was basically daring someone to do something out of the ordinary. Niddy, who thought I was about to start busting some caps, eased backward to create some space between us. I then yelled out my "PA down" battle cry, angrily pacing from side to side in front of the stunned crowd of Sevens, with my hand still in my bag.

"Fuck this shit, Muscles," Niddy said. "It's too many; let's go get the boys. Fuck these fools!" He walked down the hallway, hoping I would follow suit and do the same. But I was in a mood Niddy knew all too well, as he watched me ignore him and continue to taunt the Seven Mile kids. I pointed my hidden gun at the gang through my bag and trash talked them while they all stood stunned. Romeo knew that he had made a grave mistake by ignoring me. Even though a few of his boys had taken their pistols out of their lockers before the confrontation, none of them were in a shooting position. "Damn!" he said, reflecting on what made him ignore me in the first place.

Jerry had put the word out in the Seven Mile camp that I was neutral and not to be harmed. If it wasn't for that, I would have never been ignored. The decision to continue to ignore me was a no-brainer for the Seven Mile kids. They all smiled at me before turning around and walking down the hall to class.

While Romeo and his boys went to their classes, steamed about my wild display, Clyde and a few of his Eight Mile friends were on the third floor, settling down in the back of their black history class. The teacher, Mrs. Jenkins, passed out assignments and gave firm instructions. "I want everyone to read chapter five in silence and answer the questions at the end of the chapter; you have thirty minutes," she said.

Clyde, who was now recognized as the new Eight Mile leader, had a lot on his mind and used the thirty minutes to gather his thoughts together. Many of his friends had been kicked out of school for fighting and weapon possession. That's not counting the number of members who transferred to Ford, another school in the Eight Mile neighborhood. Even though it was every Eight Mile kid's dream to be a leader of the high-profile gang, Clyde thought otherwise. He now held the most dangerous job in Mumford; his thoughts shifted toward the Seven Mile member sitting two tables away from him: Jerry.

Just a month ago, Clyde could have easily attacked Jerry, because the Eights used to have the majority in that class. With the shift in power to the Sevens, though, he had to hold back. Clyde had watched Jerry transform from a soldier to a Seven Mile leader in a matter of weeks, and he knew if his boys didn't react to the Key-Key beatdown, they would lose a lot of respect. "Darker days are ahead," he acknowledged, while he wallowed deep in his thoughts.

Just one table away, Six Mile Jim and Matt, who were the only LAs in the class, looked concerned. They had constantly gotten angry stares from the large number of Sevens in the class since entering the classroom. Matt was visibly nervous, and it was for good reason. He usually kept a pistol on him in school, but had not brought it that day, figuring Officers Jones and Brooks were going to do a back-to-school weapons check.

Besides Jerry and Calley, the other Seven Mile members in the class were virtually unknown and itching to make a name for themselves. They wanted to prove they had enough nuts to take out the Six Mile leader and his lone companion, so they continued to stare them down.

"All you have to do is give the word, Jerry, and we'll rush them two fools," an eager Seven whispered.

"Hold up! Hold your horses. Don't nobody make a move until class is over; we got plenty of time," Jerry said with authority.

Jerry couldn't believe his new position with the BKs, but he welcomed the new power he obtained since his wild chair attack on Key-Key. He now got huge respect from Romeo and other top leaders, which gave him power over the Sevens when other leaders weren't around. Clyde, who snapped out of his deep thoughts, watched the two gang bangers closely, fearing something clearly was about to jump off. He quietly took out his small thirty-two pistol and pointed it under his table toward a few Sevens. Even though no one could see the gun under his table, he was taking a big chance. It was a chance he was willing to live with; he figured if the Sevens had enough nuts to go for a Six Mile leader after what had happened to them on the football field, anything was possible.

After forty minutes in the classroom, Matt was starting to perspire. He looked at the clock on the wall and cursed to himself when he saw he still had fifteen minutes left to go. Those fifteen minutes seemed like fifteen hours as the two Six Mile members impatiently waited for the class to end.

"What are we going to do, Matt?" Jim whispered. "Our lockers are two floors away and it's seven of them and two of us; we'll never make it!"

"Stan and some of our boys are on this floor," Matt replied. "All we have to do is somehow meet up with them when the bell rings; just don't panic, be cool."

That being said, both knew they had to run, and run at the right time, if they were going to meet up with their friends. When the bell finally rang, Matt and Jim rose quickly out of their chairs. They knew they had little time to act, so they hurried to the door, hoping to be the first out of the classroom. Unfortunately, their adversaries ran right behind them and caused a pileup in the doorway. The pileup caused a big enough wedge for Matt and Jim to slip out and race down the hallway toward Stan's class.

Jerry and his boys had no intention of letting the two get away that easy. The Seven Mile members chased Matt and Jim toward the end of the hallway like bloodhounds. Jerry drop-kicked Jim in the back of his head just as he made it to Stan's classroom, and the other Sevens followed with countless punches. Unlike Jim, Matt made it to his destination untouched, only to find out that none of his friends had made it out of the class yet. He turned around and started swinging on his adversaries, knocking one of them out with a devastating blow. The fear of being mauled from behind like Jim echoed in his mind as he swung for his life against Jerry and his friends. Yet, all the swinging in the world couldn't stop the inevitable beatdown. The Sevens circled the two kids like hungry sharks and pounded them down to the floor.

The brutalization Matt and Jim were taking was devastating, as punches turned into well-placed kicks to the body. Matt curled up like a ball and desperately tried to shield himself from the onslaught. The impact of the kicks slowed, and then seconds later the kicking stopped. Matt looked up and couldn't believe what he saw. It was Stan and a few of the boys, holding their own against his attackers. "Six o'clock," they chanted, while surprising Jerry and friends with well-coordinated punches. But Matt's smile quickly turned into a frown when he noticed about twenty Seven Mile members coming from the other way.

"Stan!" Matt yelled, hopping up from the floor like a soldier. He knew he only had seconds to act before the Sevens reached them. "Tell the boys to bail out now, dog; many more of the Sevens coming!" And then he ran from the area like he was never there.

It didn't take long for Stan and the other LAs to react to Matt's outburst; they stopped on a dime and ran toward the stairway. Jerry and company followed them, and the twenty friends Matt had seen were not far behind.

Meanwhile, Matt had made it to the first-floor entrance doors and was impatiently waiting for his friends. There was no way he was going to leave the school without knowing if they made it out, even if it took risking his own ass.

"What's taking them so long? They should've been here by now," Matt said out loud. Then all of a sudden, he saw his friends, led by Stan and Jim, running toward him from the other end of the hallway—running at top speed. Matt turned around and ran out the entrance doors. He figured Stan and the others were right behind him, but he was vastly wrong. If Matt had waited a few seconds longer, he would've seen his friends getting jumped and mauled down from behind.

Stan somehow escaped the slaughter, only to be dragged down by two Seven Mile members before he made it out the entrance doors. Stan responded by fighting like a wild animal that refused to be tamed, getting up off the floor and throwing punch after punch. His wild punches shifted the fight to the entrance, as the doors wavered in and out from the melee. Then a Seven Mile member jumped in and struck Stan with a low, swooping kick. The kick took the legs right out from under him, causing his body to flip through the entrance doors like a cowboy getting thrown out of a saloon. Three Sevens followed Stan's flying body and started kicking him just outside the school. He squealed like a pig going to slaughter as each kick got more and more violent. Matt, who was watching from behind a nearby car, ran to the scene, swinging a two-by-four at the three kids. Stan's attackers wisely run back into the school while Jim, Matt, and Stan ran from the school grounds.

Meanwhile, back inside the school, Officers Jones and Brooks had stopped the one-sided fight. The officers ran Jerry and his friends off, but not before they had injured four of the Sixes. Brooks and Jones both stared in disbelief as truant officers called ambulances to the school once more.

Soon, the school bell rang, and most of the kids were headed straight to class or their lockers. Tension consumed the hallways as students were still shaking from the horrific one-sided gang fight they had witnessed. Truant officers were everywhere, and every Six Mile member in the school walked out of class and went home after the ambulances arrived for their friends. They didn't leave because they were scared of the Sevens, though; they left because they were pissed off and wanted revenge. The Seven Mile tyranny was definitely at an all-time high. Rumors quickly spread that the now-very-depleted Eights were next on the calendar for the Seven Mile Gang.

As the hallways slowly emptied, Black Mike and Jerry headed to their last class together. All their other friends were already inside the classroom when Officers Jones and Brooks approached them.

"All right, Jerry, you're under arrest!" Officer Brooks said. "You know the routine, turn around, Mr. Tough Guy."

Jerry tried to resist, but his attempts were for nothing as the two officers aggressively wrestled him down. They arrested him in the doorway, causing onlookers in the class to throw a barrage of verbal scorn. Even the classroom teacher looked surprised after seeing a student of hers escorted away like a common criminal. P-Coal, Jerry's closest friend, was worried about his friend. Not only was he a good friend, he had become very valuable to the gang. There was no doubt that his exit would be talked about for days to come.

Elsewhere in the school, Clyde, Joey, and Big Kid, plus four other Eight Mile Gang members, were in the back of their literature class, whispering about the LAs' latest misfortunes.

"Hey Clyde, it don't look good, man," Joey said with concern. "The Sevens stomped the fuck out them Six Mile kids; they trying to take over this motherfucker … take over something we ruled for years!"

"Sit tight, Joey," Clyde said firmly. "The Sevens aren't fools, dog, remember that! We've been whipping their asses all year long, and I don't see anything changing."

"I don't think so, Clyde," Big Kid whispered. "I got to agree with Joey on this one, dog. They basically got away with murder when Jerry jumped on Key-Key; it's time to rush those hoes!"

"Both of you got to be damned fools," Clyde retorted. "In the last two months, we lost Bam-Bam, Frog, Billy, Danny, and many others. Those kids were the core of our crew; now we're just a shadow of what we once were. We can't just beat them out like we use to, and every kick-ass move we make got to be right."

The teacher, Mrs. Black, heard the kids mumbling and decided to address the matter. The gaunt-looking teacher walked to the back with authority and stopped in front of Clyde and his friends with her hands firmly on her hips.

"I want you three to be quiet!" she said. "All of you been talking since you entered my class. It's time for less talk and more work."

Clyde, Joey, and Big Kid all understood and started doing their schoolwork. All of them were good students who usually didn't talk during class. And even though the big fight was the talk of the day, the three knew completing their assignments was much more important.

Just seconds after class ended, Clyde and his friends stormed into the jubilant hallway, basically mean bugging whoever came into view. Clyde knew his top soldiers were right, even though he didn't say so out loud; the Eights were losing their grip on Mumford. It was something Clyde couldn't accept as he continued leading his boys in the hallway. His thoughts suddenly shifted, and flashes of his dead homeboy's face kept jumping into his mind. Billy and Clyde had been more than just members of the same gang. They had been real close since their Beaubian Middle School days. Clyde and Billy had first met in the Eight Mile haven school. While he thought about that first grade meeting, Clyde chuckled at the thought that even then, at the tender age of six, he and Billy were gang bangers.

His thoughts of Beaubian disappeared when he noticed more and more Eight Mile members coming to his side. By the time they reached the third floor, they were twenty-six members deep. But Clyde's mouth almost dropped to the floor when he saw all the Seven Mile members camped out in front of their lockers. Truthfully, there were about forty of them in the hallway, but the bystanders waiting to see what happened gave the appearance of many more.

Clyde stared in total disbelief. And then disbelief quickly turned into pure anger and thoughts of revenge. The Eights, led by Clyde, all ran toward the Sevens, ready to fight for their hallway. Clyde led the attack, throwing an overhand left at P-Coal, who was just turning around. The blow sent him crashing to the hard floor like a magnet. Joey and Big Kid were right behind him, swinging at the other Sevens, connecting with flurries of punches. The Seven Mile Gang outnumbered the Eight Mile Gang two to one, and after ten minutes of fighting, it started to show. While Clyde and his two friends fought on, the Eights were being virtually slaughtered right before their eyes. Although the three were holding their own, they quickly realized if they were going to survive today's fight, they were going to have to run. And ran they did. They yelled at the other members to do the same while they hurried toward the stairway.

Before Clyde ran down the stairs, he noticed Officers Jones and Brooks arriving from the other end of the hall. They were accompanied by many other officers. It was a sight that sat well with Clyde; he hated leaving the injured behind but felt much better knowing the law officials were there to rescue them.

When Clyde and his two friends opened the stairway door to the first floor, they saw two truant officers looking the other way. They quickly turned around before being noticed and went back up the stairs.

"We have to cut through the second floor and go to class from there!" Clyde said with authority.

When the three made it to the second floor, they all split up and went toward their classes. Clyde didn't worry about his friends. He knew Joey and Big Kid could handle themselves on the way to class. He did worry about the last class of the day, though—the seventh hour. It was the hour of the Sevens, an hour that had Seven Mile members in every class. Unfortunately for Clyde, his class had the most. But Clyde, who never feared any Seven Mile members, walked into the class anyway. He made eye contact with me before he sat down and sighed in relief when he noticed all the seats where the Sevens sat were empty. Clyde sat down and caressed the thirty-two pistol that still sat snuggly in his trousers. He hadn't used the pistol in the earlier hallway brawl because of all of the onlookers. Realizing the Sevens still could come through that door left him with that same dilemma ... except for one thing. He would have to shoot this time or face getting his ass beat with a gun in his lap.

"Damn, I'm in a fucked-up situation," he said quietly.

While Clyde was lost in thoughts about his sudden problem, I was across the room where most the empty chairs were. I was mulling over the fact that my grades were at an all-time low. I couldn't believe I had flunked my last assignment and realized the gang thing was taking too much of my time. Thoughts of quitting the group came to my mind while I concentrated hard on my present assignment.

When the teacher walked outside the door to look for more arriving students, Clyde left his chair and sat next to me before she stepped back inside. His sudden move startled me at first, but then I quickly realized his visit was peaceful.

"What up, dog?" he said, scooting his chair closer. "Your cousin Moe told me to tell you to holler at him after school."

"Oh yeah?" I replied. "Well, dig that, I'll give him a call; appreciate the message, Clyde."

Even though Clyde and I were from two different hoods, we both had a great deal of respect for each other. We had met in Beaubian last year during ninth grade, and Clyde recalled my one-year stay as being all too memorable. I had attended the same classes with Clyde and beefed with many of his friends that year. The young Eight Mile kids in his class back then thought I was a gang member from Six Mile. The assumption caused early problems for me at the school, because no one really knew I was a PA, who just happened to live on Six Mile Road. Clyde and Billy both kept their friends from jumping on me many times. The savior act was something I never knew about.

Suddenly, Clyde had an idea. In his mind, I owed him a favor for that protection, and he planned to collect that favor back now.

"Hey Muscles, what I'm about to say may seem kind of awkward but I need your help, dog," he said. "You see, last year at Beaubian I kept my boys from jumping you plenty times and now ... well, I'm kind of in that same situation, except my problem is with the Sevens. I was hoping you can return the favor and mob with me to my bus stop," he whispered.

"If you speak the truth, Clyde," I said, "which I think you do, I have no problem with walking with you to your stop. But what makes you think that me walking with you is going to make any difference?"

"Because when they see us together, they will automatically think our gangs are together. The Sevens would have to think twice about jumping on me then."

"Okay, okay, I hear you, but after this, that's it; we're even, Clyde, no more favors," I said firmly.

Clyde sighed in relief at my words and felt a great deal of comfort knowing I would be by his side. As the class hour wound down, I could tell Clyde was nervous. He was an easy target for the Sevens without his soldiers by his side, and it showed all over his face.

"Are you heated, dog?" Clyde asked when the bell rang.

"Nope," I said. "Officers Jones and Brooks sweated me hard right after I put it in my locker. So I asked one of my friends to get it out of the locker and mob the gun back to the hood when sixth hour ended."

"Well, don't worry; I am," Clyde replied proudly.

I looked at him and said, "Well, be ready to shoot that motherfucker if you have to, because it might come down to doing just that."

My sharp response was a reflection of how I felt about walking with a scared kid with a gun in his hand. To me, there were only two possible reasons why Clyde was reluctant to use his gun and went the scared way out. He was either scared as hell like a bitch, or he didn't want to risk losing his Mumford citizenship by shooting someone.

When we made it to the exit doors, Clyde noticed five Seven Mile members following us. Clyde and I cautiously headed out the doors. The Sevens continued to follow us, even though the small gap between us grew wider because of the crowds. We got to the parking lot but came to a complete stop when we noticed about twelve other Seven Mile members coming toward us. We stood motionless as we nervously looked around, realizing there was basically nowhere to go.

"All right, whip that bitch out, Clyde!" I yelled. "Smoke those fools in front of us, so we can make it to the bus stop, or we done!"

"You're crazy, dog! I'm not going to do no shit like that! It's too many people out here for that."

"Well, give it to me, fool!" I said, while the Sevens got closer and closer.

Clyde hesitated before nervously handing the gun to me. I, on the other hand, didn't flinch once the pistol was in my hand. I calmly checked to make sure the chamber was full, released the safety, and aimed high over the Sevens in front of us and started blasting. Everyone including the Sevens took cover; my wild aim came very close to hitting them. Actually my aim was pretty accurate because I wasn't trying to shoot anyone; I missed on purpose. Clyde's words had sunk in about shooting around bystanders. Still, I knew that we had to get to that bus stop one way or another. Clyde and I ran out of the now-empty parking lot and made it to the bus stop. We got on the bus as soon as it arrived.

A half hour later, I was just arriving home and my mind wandered back to the shooting incident. I was worried that the shooting would bring heat on my crew, but when my thoughts shifted to my temporary team-up with Clyde, I could do nothing but laugh to myself. For years the Eights and other gangs had never acknowledged the PAs as a legitimate gang. Yet, lo and behold, Clyde needed help from someone in our gang.

After standing outside a few minutes, the cold December weather chased me into my house. Once inside, I trotted to one of the three bathrooms in my house and took a well overdue leak. The three bathrooms were a luxury that low-income families from Puritan and other subdivisions didn't have. After washing my hands, I went upstairs to my room and flopped on my bed. I turned over on my back and stared at the ceiling till thoughts of school invaded my mind once more. Just then, the doorbell rang. I got out of bed and opened the window in my room. The window was located directly over my front porch. I looked out and was startled to see Niddy, Roni, and ten other PAs all jammed up on the porch.

"What up, dog? Come on down," Niddy said after seeing me stick my head out the window.

"What up, dog?" I replied. "Everybody go in the backyard, I'll be down there in a minute."

I came out the back door carrying two forty ounces of Budweiser under both of my arms, and dangling from my mouth was a bag of throwaway cups. I put the beer and the cups on a table my father used for carpentry. After giving everyone a cup of beer, I threw the empty bag in the garbage. It was not unusual for me to give cool hospitality to my friends when they came over; however, bringing beer out of my parents' house was a little too much for Z-ooh to conceive.

"Damn, dog, where you get the brew from? Aren't you worried about your people seeing you drink?" said Z-ooh.

Everybody laughed loudly at Z-ooh's comments.

"Yesterday, somebody that works at the store stole the beer and hid it behind my garage," I replied, after the laughter stopped. "So I took it and hid it inside my garage, and then I put it in the fridge when my parents went to sleep."

"What, the refrigerator? How the hell you pull that off? Your parents didn't see all that beer in the morning?" Ant-Nice asked.

"Shit, he probably hid it behind all that food. Hell, he can't even close that motherfucker without smashing a loaf of bread or something," Z-ooh added, bringing laughter once more.

Roni, who always felt at home whenever he visited, pulled out a joint and lit it up like it was legal. I couldn't hide my anger and stared at him. His boldness was unacceptable, and for a moment, I thought about checking him for it. Figuring my good friend was just caught up in the moment, I let it go.

"So Niddy," I said, "what brings you and haft of Puritan to my doorsteps?"

"A lot of members out the hood that go to Mumford have been receiving crank calls." Niddy paused before downing the last of his beer and then continued, "For some reason I think those fools from Seven Mile Road is responsible. What about you, Muscles, have you received any wild calls?"

"Nope, I just touched down moments ago. A small shoot-out at school caused me to come home late," I said.

"What? There was a shoot-out at school?" Niddy asked. "What went down?"

"Oh, nothing much," I said, downplaying the incident. "I blasted over the heads of some Sevens to get out of a tight spot."

"We all trying to figure out how those fools got all our phone numbers," said Niddy.

"I think I already know how those kids got the numbers, Niddy," I said confidently.

"For real? Tell me how."

"From your folder, nigga," I said bluntly. "You have every PA who has a phone number on your folder. To top it off, Niddy, you have all the homeys from Mumford highlighted with a marker. I'm willing to bet my last dollar that one of the Sevens seen those numbers, and the rest is history."

Niddy could do nothing but nod his head in agreement, because he knew I was right. He was careless with his folder. In fact, he probably recalled me talking shit to him and getting on his case about the folder two months ago.

"I'm glad you mentioned that, Muscles, I would've never guessed," Niddy said.

"Well, I guess that means the kid gloves are off!" Z-ooh said.

"No doubt, but what about your boy Jerry, Muscles?" Niddy said. "He parades with them motherfuckers like a Seven Mile logo, I don't like him and I don't trust him!" he said angrily.

"The cops arrested him out of school today, so we don't have to worry about him no more," I said.

"Good; now everyone listen up; I got something to say," said Niddy. "The beef with the Seven Mile Killers has just jumped on another level. To me they're nothing but hoes and they might seem like that to you too, but keep in mind, they think the same way about us. So don't underestimate them, let them underestimate you. When we're in school, don't let them crowd you, because they're deeper than us.

We got to use our head and be smart. There are going to be times when we are going to have to run, and those times are going to be the smart times."

Everyone in the backyard marveled at Niddy's speech. I always admired the glow my friend seemed to have whenever he gave a group speech. Everyone listened when Niddy spoke; sometimes even the great Uddia listened with fascination. After Niddy concluded his warning speech, the crowd of PAs seemed to be more hyper than they were all day, as chants of "PA down" could be heard all the way down the street. I was heavily involved in the chanting myself, but quickly realized the chanting in my backyard would have to stop.

"All right, the party is over," I said. "My parents will be here in a minute, so everybody got to go except for Niddy, Roni, and Ant-Nice." I motioned for everyone to leave. After giving daps and high fives to the departing PAs, Niddy and Roni, who had basketball on their minds, wondered if I felt like playing also.

"Hey Muscles, you feel like shooting ball today?" Niddy said, while motioning like he was shooting a basketball through a hoop.

"I thought we were going to go across Puritan and get paid with Boone today."

"We could do that tomorrow, Muscles; I'm not going to go to school and come back in the hood and work myself to death."

"I feel you, dog, but don't you think it would be better than freezing to death? It is pretty cold out there to be shooting some ball," I replied.

"Freeze? Man, I know you got to be kidding me, not you, not the boy who played football in the street through record-breaking temperatures," said Ant-Nice.

"You right, but that's football, we're talking about basketball now, but hey, I'm down. If it's all right with Jack, it's all right with me."

I went in the house, made everyone boloney and ham sandwiches, and grabbed my jacket. Jack, who had a hoop at his house, lived about ten houses away from me, so it was a short walk. When we arrived at Jack's house, I motioned the others to chill out in front while I knocked on his door.

When Jack opened the door and saw my face, he knew exactly what I wanted.

"Hey Jack, what's up man, you want to hoop a little bit?"

"Sure, James," Jack said in a matter-of-fact way. "Meet me in the backyard."

Jack, who was fifteen, never actually hung out with me but we knew each other. Jack was a square, but his abnormal size showed he was far from a pushover. He and I had plenty run-ins in the past and even a few fights, but we always managed to become friends again, sometimes in the same day.

"Hey everyone, he said it's all good," I yelled. We trotted through the driveway, and the first thing I did when I reached the backyard was jump and try to grab the nine-foot rim. The others followed by doing the same as soon as they entered the yard. Jack pulled his basketball out of the garage.

While everybody prepared to play, the Seven Mile kid named Cowboy was just leaving his house, heading out to look for me. He knew many of the Six Mile kids in my neighborhood and decided to make a solo visit to challenge me to a fight. He figured, if he saw me before I got across Puritan where my PA down friends were, no one would interfere in his business. Jerry and I were good friends, something Cowboy and other Seven Mile members once respected, but after the shooting, all respect was lost. All the Sevens had me on their shit list.

Cowboy's motives were backed by rumors about me that had spread before I joined up with the PA Gang. These rumors suggested I was lame and just read comic books and hung out with a bunch of nerds. Cowboy smiled to himself as he mobbed near Six Mile, wearing sagging long-pocket Levis. When he finally made it across Six Mile Road, his smile turned into gritting teeth. He saw my house but kept walking, figuring if I wasn't there, I was sure to be close by.

After walking down the street, he heard the sounds of a basketball bouncing in Jack's backyard. Cowboy followed the noise like a mouse following the Pied Piper. He reached Jack's backyard and realized that his search was finally over. After peeping out who was playing, he leaned over Jack's gate and yelled, "Next!" Cowboy knew the four Six Mile kids we were playing; they were good friends of his, and very loyal to him, even though none of them gang banged. When Niddy ended the game with a jump shot, Cowboy's old friends ran to the gate and circled around him. They all begged to play with him in the next game, hoping to get revenge.

Jack stepped aside when Cowboy came on the court. He didn't want to play with kids he didn't know that well, so he watched the game from the sidelines. Cowboy, who was noticeably larger than Niddy and me, took to the court with three of the losers from the first game. We figured this game would be much tougher, and onlookers crowded the gate to watch. Cowboy didn't just look like a ballplayer, he was a ballplayer. His height and size was an advantage, and he was known to play very physical ball.

I started the game off by taking Cowboy straight to the hole and finishing so strong around the rim, it stunned

10

A couple of days passed by since Cowboy's embarrassing defeat in Jack's backyard, and the news circulated through Mumford like wildfire. Even though I was praised with a lot of props for the fight, I still thought about quitting the gang thing. The school had sent another warning about my attendance, and failure notices continued to fill my mailbox. While I mobbed to the second floor, thoughts of my one-year stay at Beaubian came to mind once more. My most positive memory at the school had been my grades, but I was no longer getting good marks. I came to the conclusion that I seemed to focus more on my schoolwork when I had been a loner. I loved Mumford and hated the fact that my gang obligations were a major distraction.

I couldn't shake the feeling of possibly leaving the PA Gang, and I knew I had to make a decision soon. So when Niddy walked to my locker, I wasted no time talking to him about my dilemma.

"What up, Niddy? I got something to tell you, dog, something you not going to like. I'm thinking about leaving the PAs."

"What?" Niddy yelled. "Nigga, have you lost your mind? We're on the verge of taking over this bitch, and you want to quit now?"

"The shit is fucking with my grades, Niddy, and I want to graduate. This gang shit is taking me nowhere," I said bluntly.

"So you going to stop hanging with us because you don't study hard no more? Nigga, this is PA for life. If you want to quit, go ahead, dog, but you will always be a PA to me. I'm out of here; peace."

Niddy left the lockers before I could respond, obviously full of anger. I should have expected that kind of reaction.

Jenny, my god-sister, who shared lockers with me, walked up just when Niddy left.

"Hey James, hold the locker open," she said. "I'm running late for my first hour."

After she put her belongings away and left, I closed the locker and began walking to class. I knew Niddy was going to tell the others about my possible plans, and I expected the same reaction.

I entered my French class five minutes late; I frowned when I saw the teacher write it down in her books. The Seven Mile kids in the class glared at me all the way to my table. I had beaten a powerful Seven Mile figure in a fight; Cowboy was two years older than I was. It was a feat they didn't like, but a feat they respected just the same. I was also shocked to see that Niddy and Sid-Money had changed their seats. They were sitting across the room instead of next to me like they normally did.

Black Mike noticed the snub but didn't give it much thought. His thoughts, obviously, were still on my victory over Cowboy. Since Cowboy and Black Mike were good friends, revenge wasn't optional, it was a must. I saw it in Black Mike's eyes that he wanted to make me pay for the big victory … it was all about when.

While Black Mike stared at me with thoughts about attacking me, Niddy and Sid-Money were quietly discussing my talk of leaving the group.

"You really think he'd leave the crew like that, man?" Sid-Money whispered.

"I don't know, maybe," replied Niddy. "But we can't worry about him right now, dog, we got to worry about us and keep our shit tight!"

"I feel you, dog, I hear you loud and clear."

The classroom quieted down for the next thirty minutes, even though tension between the gangs was still there. Everyone in the class concentrated on the French book they were required to read, and for the first time in a while, they acted like they had some sense. But then Ronald, a Seven Mile kid who sat near Niddy, stared at him with something obviously on his mind. He wasn't a gang leader, and he wasn't a simple soldier either. He was highly touted as a fighter and was known to kick shit off anytime. Niddy returned the stares with a staredown of his own, causing nearby students to look on with interest. I noticed the staring confrontation and prayed nothing jumped off, because if it did, I would be stuck with a new dilemma: should I help Niddy or not? It was a decision I never thought I would have to make when I contemplated my plans to leave. All I really thought about was the easy concept of it, like just focusing on my schoolwork and going to class on time every day.

When the bell rang, everyone left their tables except Niddy and Ronald. They continued to stare at each other, face to face, until the French teacher yelled, "You two, get out of here!" They then rose from the tables and left the class. Ant-Nice and Sid-Money awaited Niddy, while Ronald was greeted by Black Mike and the other Seven Mile members from the class. The group of Sevens looked at the three PAs one more time, and then they walked to class like nothing transpired. The confident look on their faces angered Niddy. He wanted to make them pay for their disrespect, one way or another.

A few hours passed, and it was lunchtime; I skipped my study hour and went to lunch early just to avoid eating with the PAs. I left the line with a tray of food and headed toward a neutral table. The long table was one of the few tables that didn't have any gang influences. Usually squares and wannabes ate there.

I noticed an old friend at the table and sat next to him.

"Patrick, my boy, what's been up with you, man?" I said. "When you start going to Mumford, man? I've never seen you here."

"That's because you were too busy gang banging. Back in the day you were known to fight, but you were never into gangs," Patrick replied.

"I was banging then, Patrick," I said with a smile. "You just didn't know about it then. You have to remember, we only hung out in school, not in the streets."

"Right, right, but what about the comic books, dog? You still collect them?"

"Hell yeah, I got about a thousand of them, and that is no bullshit, my friend," I said.

"A thousand of them," Patrick said, astonished. "Damn, that's a lot of reading, dog. You always had some smarts, man, and even come from a well-off family; why you do what you do, man?"

"Because it's what I do, dog; at least it's what I did do. I'm trying to shake away from the gang banging thing, Patrick, but I'm not going to knock how I lived."

"I hear you, man, I hear you. Hey, this guy sitting across from you is Fatman. He's the jokester of the table, always looking for a laugh."

"How's it going, Muscles? What brings you to this table?" Fatman asked.

I did not respond at all. I saw right through him like he was transparent. I knew Fatman didn't like me, and I wasn't going to front like I didn't know. In many people's eyes, he was a wannabe Seven Mile Gang banger who would do anything to be accepted.

"Oh, I'm not worthy enough for a response, Mr. Six Mile James?" Fatman said with sarcasm ringing in his voice.

"You got a lot of nuts calling me that, square! You know what I represent, you know what I am … unless you just a God damn fool!" I said angrily.

This scenario was right up Fatman's alley. He knew about my fight with Cowboy and thought this would be the opportune time to get respect. He was almost twice my size and had already sized me up to be too small. Just the thought of beating the kid who beat the infamous Cowboy was enough to put glee in his eyes.

"Man, I'm not scared of you … fuck you!" he said, and then stood up out of his seat with both his fists balled.

I stared at Fatman from my seat in total disbelief and hesitated before rising myself. When I looked into his eyes, I knew he was scared. So I rode off of his fear and slapped him viciously, causing the glasses he wore to fly off his face into someone's plate. Fatman took the slap in the face like an honor, still standing with his fists balled. Everyone at the table cleared away from us after the slap, figuring a fight was imminent. I slapped him again, but this time Fatman's response was much different. He stormed to the end of the table, angry and wanting revenge. I was already at the end of the table, waiting with a punch that landed flush on his jaw. He fell backward from the blow but caught his balance and returned my punch with one of his own. I shook off the punch and threw a barrage of connecting blows to Fatman's face that left onlookers stunned. Suddenly I felt a large hand on my shoulder, causing me to turn around with a jerk. When I saw who it was, I knew the fight was over. Officers Jones and Brooks grabbed Fatman and me, and they walked us out of the lunchroom, straight to the office.

I was suspended for a week, which was so boring I was glad to return to school. I came back a few pounds heavier and one week wiser. My thoughts of leaving the group were stronger now, and being away from Niddy and the other members made my decision that much easier. I planned to move my belongings out of my locker and into a new one when first hour end. The fight with Fatman was a setback from what I really wanted …and that was to shake away from the negatives of gang violence. I let old values from my gang turn into a fight with Fatman, something I now regretted. My main objective now was to cut all relations to the Puritan Avenue life.

When I finally arrived at the lockers, I saw Jenny clearing her stuff out. I had informed her that I would be changing lockers but did not expect her to clear her stuff out until tomorrow.

"Hey sis, I thought you said you were going to clear your stuff out tomorrow," I said, bending down and helping her arrange her books.

"I have a music class to go to tomorrow," Jenny said. "So to save some time I decided to do it today."

Just as she turned and walked away, I heard some type of ranting going on down the hallway; when I turned around and looked, Ronald came into view, talking shit while Niddy, Z-ooh, and Ant-Nice followed. Apparently Ronald didn't know he was walking through the PAs' hall of lockers.

"Puritan ain't shit … fuck PA," he said as he mobbed with a swagger.

"Well, why you walking away, bitch?" Niddy said, walking fast behind him. "If we ain't shit like you say, then stop and show us what you feel, fool!"

"Fuck you! PA ain't shit," Ronald repeated as he mobbed through the hall.

But when Niddy noticed that Ronald was approaching me and my locker, he yelled at me like it was old times.

"Hey Muscles, you hear that fool? He said PA ain't shit ... get his dumb ass!"

I was already moving toward Ronald before Niddy could finish his sentence. Without hesitation, I socked the Seven Mile kid on the side of his jaw, sending him staggering into the lockers. Before I could land another punch, Z-ooh jumped in, picked Ronald up, and body-slammed him to the ground. The slam created a chain reaction from the other Puritan students in the hallway, as every one of them joined the fray. The PAs rushed Ronald like he was the last piece of bread on earth, stomping him in the hallway while pandemonium broke out. Members chanted, "PA down," after each grueling kick. The battle cry echoed through the whole school, filling students on the other floors with dread.

My friends and I booted Ronald's body around like we were kicking field goals. We stomped him down the hallway until his body bounced into a classroom. The Puritan kids followed his battered body into the classroom, where the teacher pleaded with us to stop, to no avail. We continued to stomp Ronald as the teacher screamed for help. As her screams grew louder, one by one the PAs ran out of the class. The battered Seven Mile kid was nearly unconscious when the teacher ran to his side, still yelling for help. Ronald slowly blacked out, with loud chants from the Puritan kids echoing in his mind.

Meanwhile, Niddy led all the PAs involved in the attack to the stairs; we all ran to the first floor to the locker area where the PAs from across Livernois used to hang their belongings. We stood silently for a few minutes, catching our breath and panting from the adrenalin that still ran through our veins.

"We are going to chill out here until the hallway clear, and then we going to bail up out of here. Hey Muscles, go upstairs with Z-ooh and Ant-Nice, peep out what's happening up there," Niddy ordered.

I led the two back up the stairs; we saw two truant officers walking the battered Ronald toward the counselor's office. The officers, who did not notice us, basically held up Ronald's battered body all the way to the office. When the officers disappeared from our view, I told Ant-Nice to go back downstairs to tell Niddy what we had seen. After Ant-Nice left, I looked down the empty hallway and relaxed, knowing all the kids were in class. Just seeing the quiet hallway gave me a feeling of security.

"Hey Z-ooh, fire up this haft a joint," I said. "I got some strong cologne in my back pocket, it'll kill the smell when we finish."

Z-ooh took the joint and fired it up with no hesitation. We took quick puffs off of it like it was legal, and then it was gone in a matter of seconds. Z-ooh then sprayed the hallway up with my cologne, emptying the whole bottle.

Suddenly, we heard a loud, thunderous sound coming from the other end of the hallway; when Z-ooh and I looked down the hallway, no one was there. The thunderous sound became louder and louder, and then a crowd of youngsters appeared. There were so many kids coming from the other end that Z-ooh and I both stood as if we were in a hypnotic trance.

"We need to bail up out of here now, dog," I said with urgency. "That big head motherfucker in the middle is Romeo!"

"Fuck them hoes! Those pussies ain't shit … I'm not going any where," Z-ooh replied.

I looked at Z-ooh like he was stone crazy. "Have you lost your God damn mind? It looks like it's over a hundred motherfuckers; let's leave now before they start running at us," I said.

Before Z-ooh could respond, Officers Jones and Brooks arrived on the floor from the center stairway just in time to cut off the moving mass of youngsters. Z-ooh and I ran down the stairway and rejoined Niddy and the rest of the PAs.

"We got to go, Niddy! Jones and Brooks are on the second floor," I warned.

"Yeah, I know," he said. "We seen them go up the stairs, but they didn't see us; let's go."

We all ran down the hallway and out of the school like the building was on fire. Running with a full head of steam, we reached the bus stop in seconds, and five minutes later, the twelve of us boarded the bus like a brigade coming home from a war.

I stared out the window with bitterness and sorrow, feeling stupid for being part of the humiliation of jumping only one kid. At the same time, though, I thought Ronald was even more stupid. I knew that as good as I am in a fight, I would've never done what Ronald did. Ronald had broken the rule of all rules, and that was to never disrespect a crew in their own hall. I took no comfort over Ronald's stupidity, as thoughts of quitting the gang went straight out the window.

It became unusually quiet on the bus; normally after a fight there was all sorts of trash talking going on; this quietness unnerved me. It was a long ride home.

When the bus finally arrived in the hood on Puritan Avenue, the twelve of us left the bus laughing with big smiles on our faces. We all knew we had just dodged a bullet, and we were obviously happy to make it home.

11

After the jumping of Ronald in school, another day of violence was expected. Fifteen PAs, including Little Robby, a twelve-year-old member, boarded the Dexter bus while carrying thirteen guns. We had plans to make the Sevens pay for running us out of the school, and at the same time we knew the Seven Mile Gang was planning to get back at us for what happened to Ronald. Six of the members on the bus didn't attend Mumford, and Niddy was worried about how they would get inside. Officers Jones and Brooks always checked for weapons and IDs at the entrance doors, so the plan had to be right. Suddenly, he had an idea that he thought just might work.

"Hey Little Robby, I have a job for you, a job you'll like better than just being a lookout for us," he said.

"Oh yeah?" he said. "What is it?"

"When we get off the bus and go to the school, I want you to carry Muscles's gym bag," Niddy said with a smirk.

"That don't seem to be such a big deal," Little Robby replied.

"That's because I didn't tell you what's in the bag, kid. We have thirteen guns that got to get in that school, and they in that bag you're going to carry," Niddy said bluntly. "So can you handle the job or not?"

Little Robby was Niddy's little cousin; he had begged to come along so much that Niddy finally let him. He was hoping for a bigger role in Niddy's plan and welcomed the job of carrying the guns.

"Hell yeah, I'll do it; I'll even shoot if you want me to," he said.

"Naw, dog," Niddy replied. "You ain't got to worry about that part. All I want you to do is carry the bag into the school."

When the bus stopped, the PAs all got off, with one thing on our minds: to take care of business. We didn't plan to shoot anyone; we just wanted to intimidate our enemies and give them a taste of what would happen if they got out of line in the future. Everyone knew what to do once we made it inside, but getting in undetected was the problem.

When we neared the entrance doors, we split up and mingled into the crowd while Little Robby snuck in the side door. The six PA kids who didn't attend the school also got in with no problem, as Officers Jones and Brooks overlooked them and focused on the Mumford students. Once everyone was in the building, Niddy and the crew of PAs went straight to work. Travis was the first to grab a gun from the bag, pulling out his thirty-two automatic with the hair-trigger pin. Everyone else followed and did the same as Little Robby discreetly held the bag. After everyone grabbed a gun, the PAs that were from the hood ran to the end of the hallway while the rest of us ran up the stairs.

When we made it to the second floor, we hurried toward the Seven Mile lockers with rage glowing in our eyes. However, when we got to the lockers, we were surprised to see only four Seven Mile members in the hall. The Sevens turned around with fear painted all over their faces, and it was quite obvious who the paint brushes were. Niddy, Uddia, and I ran up to Grimace, who was the biggest Seven

Mile member in the school, with balled fists. We intimidated him with PA battle cries; he did nothing but walked away from us and hurried out of the hallway toward the stairs. The other three members did the same when the rest of the PAs showed them their guns.

Travis was pacing impatiently on the first floor, waiting for Niddy and the others to return. Timing was the key, and the longer the non-Mumford students waited, the bigger the chance they would get caught. Rally, Roni, Big-Ant, Big-Tone, and Little Robby were the other non-Mumford students.

Meanwhile, Grimace and his three Seven Mile friends were halfway down the stairway when they heard Niddy and the rest of us entering the stairs. Grimace thought once they made it to the first floor, they would be home free.

The four Seven Mile students crashed open the doors to the first floor, knocking down two kids in the hall. What was waiting for them outside that door, though, was a real situation to deal with.

Travis and the five other PAs attacked Grimace and his friends in the small corridor like mobsters, striking them with their pistols. Grimace tried to fight, but when Niddy and the others arrived behind him, they started swinging their pistols too. Grimace was able to cover up pretty well because of his size, but the toll of being struck by cold iron started to wear. His friends, who hid behind him like he was a human shield, were also beaten by the pistols. The two-minute pistol-whipping was enough for them to realize they had to get the hell out of the hallway and soon. Suddenly the pistols stopped flying like they were never flung.

My PA friends and I ran to the front doors, pushed them open, and ran like never before. Officers Jones and Brooks saw us running and headed to the doors, but we were gone when they got there. The officers took out walkie-talkies and

When we made it back to the hood, it was like a breath of fresh air. Everyone sighed in relief when we crossed Puritan Avenue, and jokes and loud laughter followed.

"Man, the Sevens didn't stand a chance against us," Z-ooh said proudly. "I'll fight one of them chumps any day!"

"Ha! The funniest thing about it was … most of them motherfuckers didn't come to school today," said Robin.

"All right, all right, let's not get too cocky," said Niddy. "The reason they didn't come to school is because they were probably planning something major."

"I agree," Uddia said bluntly. "Stay on your guard tomorrow; they won't take what happen today lying down."

For the moment, we were happy and feeling like we had gotten away with the biggest crime on earth, but when everyone went to sleep that night, it was a totally different thing. Everyone knew when they got up in the morning to go to school, it was going to be a different day. It was all about whose day will it be this time, whose day?

The next day, when Black Mike and Romeo entered the school, they were mad and furious as hell. Yesterday's pistol-whipping by the PAs was all over the school, and revenge was definitely a must. What was bigger news was the discovery of Jerry's recent visitors. Some kids in Jerry's neighborhood saw the fifteen PAs coming into and leaving his house, and the word had made it back to the Seven Mile camp. Nobody from the Seven Mile Gang talked to Jerry since the discovery, and none of them had plans to; he was at the top of their shit list.

Most the Sevens had taken the previous day off to regroup and make plans for an attack in school; they had no idea the PA Gang was going to beat them to the punch. Now the school officials were prepared for such an attack, and security was at an all-time high again. Black Mike and Romeo both agreed that revenge this time would have to be carried out in the street. While the Sevens went to their lockers with angry faces, the Eight Mile Gang on the third floor had smiles on theirs. The depleted gang had been pleased to see their archenemies fall and planned to take advantage of their misfortunes soon. The Six Mile Gang had been so delighted about the Sevens' drama that they had thrown a party last night. The Seven Mile Gang had become so unlikable in Mumford that even non-gang members wanted to see them go down.

After three hours of tense class work, the gangs once more crowded the halls of the school. Although there was no drama or altercations in the classrooms, violence was still possible in between classes.

Niddy and I walked cautiously through the hallway, trying to make it to our lockers; we knew we were easy targets. We felt better when we noticed Ant-Nice coming out of his classroom. He quickly joined us on the journey through the crowded hallway, prepared for anything to happen, already peeping out the situation.

Suddenly, an unknown Seven Mile member deliberately bumped into me and almost knocked me down from the impact. It was so unexpected that all three of us were stunned for a few seconds while he continued to walk like he hadn't done anything. I followed him all the way to his locker and shoved him hard against the wall. Niddy and Ant-Nice both followed me like they were heading to death row. They knew that going into the Seven Mile locker area was dangerous, but they had to make sure I didn't walk into a fucked-up situation by myself.

The unknown kid acted like he wanted to fight, balling up his fists after I pushed him, but he backed away when I started to swing. Niddy and Ant-Nice stopped me from hitting him. They wrestled me away from the lockers and hurried me out of the hallway when they noticed two truant officers at the end of the hall.

"What the fuck you do that for?" I said after I calmed down

"A short fuse ain't what we need right now, dog," Niddy replied. "We got to be smart. The whole school is watching us and waiting like a motherfucker for us to fuck up soon. Besides, if you keep getting into fights and going to the office, you can forget all about graduating from here."

Niddy's words hit home like a lightning bolt striking a tree. Just the mention of the word *graduation* was enough to make me forget about the Seven Mile kid. Graduating from school was still my number one priority, and since it was Niddy's and Ant-Nice's too, we would all go out of our way to keep focused on that goal.

"You're right, Niddy," I said. "We got a long two years to go, and at the pace of battles we're going through, we'll never see that stage … unless we stay smart."

"Let's be realistic," Ant-Nice added. "The drama we go through every day is not going to let us be smart. Just the fact we got to defend ourselves every day from bullshit like that," he stopped and gestured toward where the altercation took place, "tell the whole story."

"We still got to try, Ant, we still got to try; remember, the object to come to school is to learn, boy!" Niddy said, with sarcasm ringing in his voice.

A large number of PA kids were camped out at the lockers, impatiently waiting for us. The gathering at the lockers between classes continued for the remainder of the day as danger lurked in the shadows each hour.

That Saturday morning was sunny but cold. The winter glow woke me up, causing me to hurry out of my bed straight to the window; I could see it had snowed when I looked through my drapes. Marveling at the beautiful view, my thoughts quickly started to wander. I thought about the fights and beefs we had all week, and most of all I wondered when the Sevens were going to strike. The past few days in school had been quiet, but many near altercations in the street proved an attack was imminent. But it was the weekend, and thoughts of today's agenda pushed those thoughts right out of my mind.

I left the window, started my bath water, and then called Roni. We talked for a minute and decided to meet up and then head across Puritan. After I took my bath and put on some fresh clothes and a warm coat, I ran down the spiral stairs. As I trotted to the front door, the phone rang. When I answered it, I was a little shocked to hear who was on the other end.

"What's up, Jerry? What's going on?" I said, not hiding the surprise in my voice.

"What up, dog? My boy want some weed, I was wondering if you could do me a favor and cop me some."

"Sure, but you going to have to meet me across Puritan, because I suppose to hook up with Roni today. Meet me at Niddy's."

"Bet, I'm leaving right now," he said, before hanging the phone up.

I left the house wondering who that friend was. I hurried up the street to meet Roni. Since Roni lived on the third block from my house, we would usually meet each other in the middle of the second block. While I walked, I looked at the houses on the street. Each house I passed by was nice, but every one of them seemed to get less and less attractive. I never understood why the houses and neighborhoods started dramatically changing toward Puritan. The houses across Puritan were small wooden houses compared to the large brick houses on my side. There were vacant lots all over the neighborhood from where houses used to be. You were stepping into a total different world when you stepped across Puritan Avenue.

I met up with Roni, and the two of us mobbed across Puritan, walking in the street instead of the snow-filled sidewalk. The neighborhood was too poor to pay men to shovel the sidewalks every time it snowed. Only the rich and middle class neighborhoods could afford such luxuries.

After walking one block across Puritan and then crossing Midland Road, Roni and I saw Niddy, shoveling snow off his sidewalk. When we reached him, he was touching up his porch and just finishing up his sidewalk.

"You're shoveling that snow like you want to go make some money or something," I said.

"Naw, dog, it ain't thick enough or high enough; that's why I was able to knock this out so quickly," Niddy replied.

"It supposed to snow heavy tonight," Roni said, "so it ought to be hellee money out there tomorrow."

"I don't know about that, Roni," I said. "The base heads and the dope fiends are going to be out there too."

"Fuck them dope heads," Niddy said bluntly. "All they're going to do is shovel one house and then rush back to the hood to buy some rocks."

Laughter followed Niddy's statement, but as shrewd as it may have sounded, I knew he was right. There were rock heads in neighborhoods all over Detroit. They would steal, rob, and in some cases even sell themselves. There was nothing a rock head would not do for money.

"Hey Niddy, what's up with Boone? Are we working with him tomorrow or what?"

"I don't know, Roni, if it snow like you say it suppose to, we stand a better chance of getting paid with a shovel."

"I agree," I said. "I rather shovel snow anyway; I don't care too much for selling the rock."

"Yeah, that's easy for you to say, because you don't have to really roll, nigga."

"You right," I said, "I don't really have to. That's why I don't roll as much as you cats, but I'm here to tell you that's not why I rather work than sell rocks. At first it was fun, you know, getting paid, pulling top notch hoes and shit, and then something dawned on me more than the money and hoes, and that was the destruction of our own people. Every rock I sold was to someone in my own race, something I am not proud about."

"I never looked at it like that, Muscles; all I looked at was the motherfucking green."

Roni laughed at Niddy's remarks, but I didn't crack a smile. Every time I talked about demographic issues to my PA friends, my rhetoric would always be dismissed in the form of jokes.

After Niddy put his shovel in the garage, we headed to Uddia's house down Midland Road. While we walked, thoughts of Jerry's phone call kept jumping in and out of my mind. I knew he more than likely would be coming to the hood with a friend I didn't know. Since Jerry had met the major core of my group in his basement, I figured the two outlanders would be safe in the hood until I saw them.

Just before we turned down Uddia's street, a chubby fifteen-year-old kid named Bernie saw us and begged to come along. He was a PA kid who would do anything to be accepted in the hood as a gang banger. He pleaded to come with us as we continued walking, ignoring him as if he was not even there. Bernie came along any way, figuring it was all good since we hadn't said he couldn't come.

When we got to Uddia's house, Niddy knocked on the door. Uddia appeared in the doorway with the demeanor of a king about to address his people. If he was your friend, it was a very good thing, but if he wasn't, it could be a very bad thing. The first person Uddia noticed when he opened the door was a gleeful looking Bernie.

"Where you get this bitch from? When PAs start hanging with hoes?" he said, not expecting an answer.

Bernie ignored Uddia's humiliating comments and continued to smile.

"Stop smiling, bitch," Uddia said after stepping out of the doorway to the porch.

It was obvious Uddia didn't like Bernie; top reason, he was too scared to fight or do anything violent. That was unacceptable in the gang bang world. Uddia went inside and came back out with a long coat on, ready to go. We all left his block and walked to the Candy Store, going behind the building. Rally was already back there, chilling out on the back steps, smoking a joint. He greeted us with hugs and daps. We all puffed on the weed and joked around like a bunch of silly kids instead of teenagers. Then the jokes started to get physical as Uddia chose to fuck with Bernie to test him.

"Hey Bernie, you've been smoking our weed and talking shit like you're a PA boy. Well, it's time you earned the right to be down, nigga. I want you to wrestle Roni, and I want you to do it now," he ordered.

The command to fight was surprising but not unexpected, because everyone knew Uddia would challenge anyone, anytime, to individual battles. In fact, he took personal joy in seeing others physically wrestle each other.

"Leave me alone, Ude; I don't feel like it."

"What?" Uddia yelled. "If you don't wrestle him, you going to have to wrestle me, fool."

The chubby kid wanted no part of Uddia, but he was still reluctant to get in the square with Roni. Roni, on the other hand, stared at Bernie like he was a piece of chopped liver ready for the grinding.

"What the fuck you scared for, Bernie? It ain't like we're fighting, we just wrestling," he said.

"I just don't feel like it, dog; I don't like wrestling."

Uddia suddenly struck Bernie on the side of his face with an open-palmed slap. The momentum from the impact sent Bernie tumbling into Roni, like Uddia planned. Subsequently, Roni grabbed Bernie and slung him into the building like he was a rag doll. After falling to the ground, Bernie panicked and let out a slight scream, fearing he was about to get jumped. But everyone behind the building laughed instead of attacking him.

Bernie's troubles were far from over as Uddia collared him up from the ground like he was grabbing a pit by its coat. This time he deliberately threw him into Niddy, hoping Niddy would respond physically. And he was right. Niddy picked Bernie up and body-slammed him as soon as contact was made.

"Wrestle Niddy, fool," Uddia said, while Bernie whimpered on the ground, refusing to stand on his feet. "Being part of us means you can never back down from no one in a one-on-one confrontation. The only way you can be down is to *be* down."

The phrase "be down" echoed in Bernie's head as he slowly got up from the ground. An overwhelming fear radiated from his body. He lunged at Niddy with the thought of slamming him, only to get slammed himself. He got up from the ground with pure determination, as tears started to stream from his eyes. This time he lunged at Niddy with an animallike growl that surprised even the great Uddia. Unfortunately, Bernie was bested again as Niddy's body-to-body slam took the life out of him, causing him to lay still on the ground. I stared at the sideshow like I was looking at a horror movie. I didn't like how they were bullying Bernie, nor did I like the fact that Bernie willingly put himself in this situation. More PA kids flocked to the wrestling scene, going behind the building like it was the biggest show on earth.

This was the time I thought I should make my exit. I had seen enough. "I'm out of here, Ude; me and Roni going to mob to my house and meet a friend of mine's; I'll be back," I said.

Roni followed me out from behind the building. He knew I really didn't like being around bullshit.

While walking down Puritan, my thoughts quickly turned to Jerry. I figured about the time he made it to his house near Six Mile Road, I should be just arriving at the Dexter bus stop on Fairfield. Although I had instructed Jerry to meet me at Niddy's house, I felt I could catch him at the bus stop before he started that journey.

When we got back to my house, Jerry was nowhere to be seen. I found out from my neighbors he already had been by and was last seen going toward Puritan with a friend. Roni and I stood on my porch and pondered Jerry's whereabouts, and then we walked inside.

12

After Jerry left my house, he headed to the candy store with Calley. Jerry figured that was where I would be if I wasn't at Niddy's house. While the two nervously walked toward their destination, Jerry's thoughts quickly turned to Calley. Before he had called me, he had found out some disturbing news about his friend. He found out Calley was the one responsible for his recent fallout with the Seven Mile Crew. A reliable source told Jerry that Calley snitched on him to get credibility in the crew. It was an action that would not go unnoticed. Jerry had plans for Calley, plans that consisted of pain and agony.

When they arrived at the candy store, goosebumps immediately ran up and down their bodies, as fear shook them both. They knew they were taking a chance by coming into the PAs' stronghold, but Jerry was counting on running into me or some of my friends that were in his basement last week. Coincidently, the first person Jerry noticed when he entered the store was Uddia. He told Calley to wait by the door and walked up to Uddia while he was playing an arcade game.

"Hey what's up, Uddia? I'm Jerry, remember me? I'm the kid who let you and your friends cool out in my basement."

"Yeah, I remember. What's up, and what bring you to the heart of our hood?"

"I was informed to meet my boy Muscles at Niddy's to buy some smoke, but that's not important now; what's important is the Seven Mile snitch I brought for you guys."

"Seven Mile snitch? Aren't you part of they crew, fool? Why would you bring one of your own boys to a danger zone?"

"Because he set me up and the Sevens don't give a damn about me now; they put a Seven Mile hit out on me."

"He got any money?" Uddia said with curiosity.

"Most definitely, but bigger than that, he got some fresh ass hiking boots on his feet."

Uddia paused and stopped playing the game, and then he stared at Jerry from head to toe and said, "Your shoes are fresh too … in fact, your shoes look better."

Little Norm and the others laughed so loudly, everyone in the store turned and looked in that direction.

"I'm just fucking with you, dog; you Muscles' boy, I don't want your shoes," Uddia said. "Tell your boy we got some weed and we will meet him on the corner; we will take care of him from there."

Jerry hurried out of the candy store, with Calley by his side, and did exactly as Uddia told him. They waited on the corner, and after about five minutes, Uddia, Niddy, Little Norm, and Bernie came out of the store and went to the corner. Uddia then motioned everyone to follow him to the alley. When they got behind the building, all hell broke loose. Little Norm socked Calley in his eye from his blind side and demanded he give up his boots while everyone else stepped back. The surprise attack caught Calley clearly off guard, but it was not enough to make him fall or give up his boots. Instead, he tried to fight back, even though he saw Uddia and the others standing and waiting like wolves in the shadows.

Little Norm and Calley fought in the snow like cats and dogs. When Little Norm realized he wasn't going to be able to take his shoes, he decided to do the next best thing: he pulled out his pistol. He smacked Calley around with the pistol like he was whipping a dog with a rolled-up newspaper. Calley did nothing but take the punishment with his fists and elbows tucked tight by his waistline. In the midst of the pistol-whipping, he thought about trying to take the weapon away from him but quickly dismissed the idea when he saw the rage in Little Norm's eyes. Unlike Bernie, Little Norm never hesitated to fulfill one of Uddia's orders. He was the brother of Z-ooh, and today he officially became part of the PA family.

While Calley was falling to the wrath of Little Norm, I was back home, saying my good-byes to Roni. My father had sent Roni home because he wanted to have a much-needed talk with me. He had watched my destruction far too long to stand by any longer. My father was a well-respected, articulate artist who wanted me to follow in his footsteps and be successful in life. He wanted to send me to the best college when I graduated and was prepared to provide me with anything I needed to fulfill that goal. Because of this, most kids thought I was spoiled, but they failed to realize that my father had worked hard for everything he got and made it a major priority to instill the same ethics in me.

"James, it's about time we have a talk, son," my father said after I closed the front door. "Your grades have been dropping, and you're hanging in them streets more than you are at home, plus you're worrying your mother a lot."

"I'm going to do better, Dad … I promise," I said sincerely.

"I hope so, son, or I'm going to have to result to drastic measures if the streets prevent you from graduating and getting an education. I told you many times that I will buy you a car if you graduate, but keep in mind if you don't, I'm not buying you shit."

"Okay, Dad, I get the message. I'm going to go out my way to make sure nothing distracts my two-year mission to graduate."

"You're saying that like you doing me a favor or something, son; I'm telling you this for your own good, not mine. What you don't understand is when I was your age, I was so poor that I swore I would never live like that when I grew up. It took hard work, though, something your generation seems to know nothing about. In my time, black people had to work twice as hard to get somewhere in life. Now that times are much better, people from the old days try to give their children the things they could never give them when they were young. Some kids appreciate it, but obviously some don't and continue to live like times were always equal. That is why I have no problem with your friends, and you shouldn't either. I know they are poor and have a bigger disadvantage than you, but they got to find they own way like I did, and that means working twice as hard. But not you, James; no, not you, you're not poor, and you have no disadvantages. There should be no excuses for you not to succeed in anything you want to achieve." When my father finished his comments, he left the room.

I felt numb from his words; I was completely awestruck by my father's remarks. I didn't bother to get up from my seat; instead I sat five more minutes, pondering everything my dad had just said. I wondered if I could commit to the obligation my father demanded. While I thought about my father's comments, the doorbell rang and I quickly snapped back to reality. When I looked out the door, I gasped. Jerry was standing there with a very bloody, battered kid I could not recognize.

"Man, what the fuck happen to him, dog?" I asked. "Who the fuck is he?"

"It's Calley; remember him? He's the guy who got his shoes took at the bus stop; well … it happened again. Only this time he got his shoes took over here," said Jerry.

After they entered the house, I directed them to the den, and then I got some ointment and Band-Aids. Sadly, all the Band-Aids in the house wouldn't have covered Calley's wounds; the open gashes in his head continued to bleed.

"Man, this boy needs a doctor," I said, while trying to stop an open wound from bleeding with a damp rag.

"I'm straight, dog," Calley said nervously. "I'm not fucking with any hospitals."

"You should, man, it doesn't make sense to bail back to your hood like this," I said with concern.

"He's right, Calley; you should at least let us call you an ambulance," Jerry added.

"I can do better than that, dog," I said. "I could ask my moms to take you right now!"

"Thanks, but I think I'll be fine. I appreciate the Band-Aids and shit, but it's time for me to go now. Peace."

Calley left the den and walked to the front door, obviously ready to leave, but he stopped short of opening the door and waited for me to do that. Jerry, who was right behind him, giggled out loud when I let Calley out. Calley turned around and stared coldly at Jerry. I noticed the exchange but couldn't understand why Jerry thought the matter was so funny; how could he laugh at his friend like that?

"Why were you laughing at your boy, Jerry?" I asked after I closed the door. I walked away from him and went into the den to pick up the phone.

"That motherfucker snitched on me, so I set his bitch ass up with your boys across Puritan," he said, following me into the den. He paused and giggled again. "Little Norm pistol-whipped the shit out of that punk …who are you calling?"

"The ambulance, stupid, your friend didn't walk toward the bus stop, which means he must be going to try to walk all the way home. The shape he's in, he'll never make it, so I'm calling an ambulance for him, okay?"

"Man, fuck that dude! He is from Seven Mile, remember? You shouldn't give a damn about him; hell, you don't even know him that well; why do you give a fuck, man?"

"If you had a problem with him, Jerry," I said, still holding the receiver, "why didn't you just handle it? Why didn't you fight him one on one or pistol-whip him yourself? You had to bait my boys in with money, because I know them well and I know it's going take more than some gym shoes and a big mouth to get them going."

"Why you tripping, dog? You suppose to be my boy, I just told you the fool snitched on me."

"I don't like the way you handle business, Jerry. You are a manipulator, and you are wrong, now shut up for a minute while I call your friend an ambulance."

Jerry looked at me coldly as I told the operator where to send the ambulance. He didn't expect me to react like that. He had considered me a good friend and couldn't recall the last time he saw me this mad. But being called "stupid" and being told to shut up didn't sit well with Jerry, so he decided to leave.

"I'm out of here, dog, I catch up with you later," he said as he left the house. I did not respond at all to him and continued to talk to the operator.

When I hung up the phone, it seemed like a million different thoughts attacked my mind at once. Only one thought dominated, though, and that was Jerry's treachery.

I thought Jerry was not only a manipulator, he was a shit starter. Subsequently, I thought the differences between our rival gangs would grow wider because of this fact. I didn't like the gang from Seven Mile Road, but I strongly respected my values of right and wrong. Although I had fought with gangs and sold drugs in the street, I had never stolen, robbed, or killed anybody.

My train of thought became derailed when my father yelled for me to come down to the basement. I left the den after hearing his familiar call. The interruption was much appreciated; I knew whatever he wanted me to do would take my thoughts away from Jerry.

Meanwhile, Black Mike and other Seven Mile leaders were spending their Saturday evening at Hampton field. The Seven Mile haven school had the atmosphere of a packed fair as kids from all around the area crowded the schoolyard with radios and coolers full of pop and beer. The strong smell of reefer lurked in the air, and young girls crowded the open parking lots, dancing to the latest gangster rap songs. All the young gang members in Detroit loved gangster rap, while youngsters who weren't into gang activities mostly listen to traditional hard rap. Nevertheless, the sounds from the radio had everyone at Hampton loud and hyped.

While everyone in the schoolyard seemed to be in a good mood, the look on Black Mike's face told another story. He was still angry about the gang's most recent setback, the embarrassing pistol lashing of his close friend Grimace, who was so embarrassed by the incident, he didn't bother to show up at the playground. Black Mike didn't blame the big guy. He had been humiliated.

Black Mike's thoughts returned to the day before that tragic beatdown. He had warned his friend not to go to school that morning. He told him to stick with the plan like everyone else, and that was to take a day off and come back with a bang the next day. Instead, he didn't listen and became a victim of the PAs. His jumping caused all the Seven Mile leaders to reschedule that next day's bang plan and focus on the core of their problems: the PA Gang. The names of Wee and his pal Chuck were circulating through the Seven Mile neighborhood, and so was Niddy's. Niddy's name came up because of his involvement in the Grimace fight, and his name was spray-painted in every bathroom, which didn't help either.

Although Niddy was at the top of Black Mike's shit list, he was ready to settle for the second big fish, which in his eyes was Wee. Black Mike and a few close friends planned to pay the Livernois PA leader a visit at the Mercury Theater. The movie theater was a hangout for inner city gangs around the area of Six Mile and Schaefer. Recently, Wee and Chuck had been leading victorious gang fights in and outside the theater. Their pattern of fighting every weekend was quickly recognized by their adversaries.

After an hour of socializing and having some fun, Black Mike led thirty-five members out the schoolyard and ordered about half of them to go with him to the Mercury. The hyped-up command was sharp and direct. Seventeen kids crowded into four cars and peeled out of the parking lot like a drag race. Black Mike was in the first car, which was an old-school white Caprice; this car was followed by two Impalas and a Dodge. The four cars traveled toward the theater with loud tail pipes that echoed through the hood.

Meanwhile, across the street from the Mercury, Wee and ten friends were just finishing eating at the Coney Island. Before leaving the restaurant, they played arcade games before walking to the bus stop, just in time to board the bus. Wee was concerned; despite his warning, five of his friends had stayed in the theater to watch another movie. He knew they could handle themselves, but he still couldn't stop worrying. As the bus pulled away from the curb, the four cars with the Seven Mile members in them turned the corner. They drove to the back parking lot, parked their cars, and headed to the front of the building.

When they reached the front of the theater, they lined up in a single file and bought their tickets. Since the movie had already started, the manager wasn't going to let them into the lobby. But after making a lot of noise and complaining that they didn't want to come back later, the manager gave in and let them in the building. Black Mike and Cowboy led the way into the lobby as two ticket sellers stared at the group of kids like they were walking danger signs.

After goofing around at the refreshment bar, Black Mike motioned everyone to follow him into the movie area. The gang of teenagers looked down each row of seats for Wee and his friends, but they didn't see anybody. They all sat down in the back of the theater, where the chairs were higher and the view was better.

"I'm going back to the snack bar," Black Mike said as soon as he sat down. "I need seven of you to come with me; the rest can chill here."

Black Mike rose out of his chair with an aura of authority and led the seven others back to the refreshment bar. When they got in line, they saw four PAs at the arcade machines. Their eyes lit up. Without thinking, every Seven Mile member ran to the arcade area and attacked the PAs while their backs were turned. Each of the PAs fell to floor from the onslaught, and ruthless kicks followed afterward. The ushers tried to stop the slaughter but failed to prevail as the rest of the Seven Mile members rushed to the lobby. The intervention by the ushers distracted the crowd of Sevens coming to the scene, creating enough breathing room for the four battered PAs to run out of the building. The Seven

Mile members followed them toward Meyer's Road before giving up and ending the chase.

13

Monday morning was quiet and had the smell of winter when I looked out my window. It wasn't the average Monday, I thought while inhaling and exhaling the cold air through my nostrils. It had been two days since the Calley robbery and the PA beatdown at the Mercury. I rubbed my chin and knew there would be repercussions on both sides.

I closed the window, took my clothes out, and laid them on the bed. Then I took a quick shower, brushed my teeth, and came back to my room. I heard someone knocking at my door while I was putting on my pants; I trotted to the window and opened it again. When I looked outside the window, I was surprised to see Niddy, Z-ooh, Sid-Money, and Ant-Nice waiting on my porch.

"We running late, dog, we was hoping to get a ride with you and your moms this morning," Niddy said.

"I'm pretty sure it's cool, man …just hang on a minute. I'll be right down."

I already knew the answer, but I asked my moms if they could come with us; after she said yes, I went out of the house with the keys to her car, a blue 82 Cougar. The five of us waited in my mom's car in total silence. The drama in school was becoming so common that fights had become expected. What we might face in school today was on everybody's mind, and it showed.

My mom hurried out of the house and quickly drove us to Mumford. We got out of the car, expecting drama on the way to the doors, but there wasn't any, and we entered the building. Sid-Money was the only member armed with a gun, and he was taking a big risk by carrying it. But since we were running late to school, most of the kids were already in class, and security was light. Niddy led the way to the lockers; the empty hallways were silent without the noise of students. Sid-Money quickly put his gun in his locker and sighed, grateful to get the gun out of his hands. After we put our coats in the lockers, we headed to our first hour class.

Fifty-five minutes later, the bell rang and students flooded the hallways trying to get to their lockers and their next class. The PAs had other intentions, though, as we crowded the opposite side of the Seven Mile Gang's hallway. Niddy had put the word out in class to meet there, and members showed up one by one. Few Seven Mile members walked by, and we ridiculed the ones who did. This angered Black Mike and the other members, causing them to watch us closely. The surprise seizure of the hallway and the ridiculing of his friends clearly caught him off guard. By the time the second bell rang, every PA member was at the end of that hall.

"Man, I'm ready to swing on them hoes right now," I said. "What the fuck are we waiting for?"

"Chill out, Muscles, we going to wait for the right time, only then we attack, okay?" said Niddy. "We just can't do shit without thinking, we got to be organized."

"Yeah, well, while you trying to organize, the Sevens pumping up a plan how to use those big numbers they have on us."

"He's right, Niddy," Ant-Nice said, after noticing more and more Seven Mile members arriving to the scene. Even though the halls were clearing out, the two gangs stayed crewed on both ends of the hall, staring at each other.

Surprisingly, Clyde and twelve of his Eight Mile friends came to the scene and joined the PAs in the hall. Clyde saw the hallway seizure as an opportunity to get his crew back in the spotlight, but Niddy thought his antics portrayed him like a hoe. He didn't respond to them when they shook hands with me and the others. In fact, he went out of his way to snub Clyde when he approached him for a handshake. Clyde took the snub with a smile.

Eventually, the PAs grew much more hyper.

"Fuck this shit, dog," I said, "I'm going down there, and I'm going now!"

I left the crew of gang bangers without even looking back, ignoring Niddy's pleas to wait. When I reached the Seven Mile Gang lockers, the twenty-something members in the hallway looked at me like I was crazy. Those looks, however, turned into frowns when they noticed the gang of PAs that followed behind me. Even Clyde and his boys, who also mobbed to the end of the hallway, had fighting on their minds. The two-to-one odds were rare for the PAs, and we outnumbered the Sevens since more and more of their members had stayed home from school again.

Instead of attacking the outnumbered Seven Mile Gang, who did not want to fight, we shoved some of them into the lockers and heckled them with PA down chants. The chants were so loud that Clyde and his friends, who stood and watched the onslaught, refused to holler their own hood. It was as if the Eight Mile Gang was trying to show respect to Puritan. Black Mike avoided all confrontations and ran down the nearest stairway, hoping his friends would follow suit. And follow him they did, but it wasn't because of Black Mike's exit. It was because of Officer Jones and ten law officials storming to the scene. The officials cleared the hallways with strong-arm scare tactics that would make anyone run. They threw some of the youngsters to the floor like they were animals, and then purposely let them go and allowed them to run.

After the clear-out, my friends ran out of the school, fearing they would be apprehended later. It was the second time in less than ten days we had to run out of the building.

Niddy and I got to school the next day three hours late. We had attended a late-night celebration across Puritan the previous night, and the party had taken a toll on us. This time we took the bus to school instead of getting a ride from my moms, and it was just two of us instead of five like the day before. Most of the other PAs stayed at home, fearing the law officials would try to detain them if they came. The situation was different with Niddy and me, though. We both wanted to come because of our weak attendance in class. During the ride to school, Niddy and I both wanted to turn around and go back home, but we didn't because of pride.

After third hour class, some kids hurried to make it to the lunch line before it got crowded. The atmosphere in the hallways was quiet, something unusual for one of the most dangerous schools in Detroit. However, no one took the quietness for granted, especially knowing anything could happen anytime in Mumford. The few PAs who came to school piled up at the back of the lunch line and waited for the lunch doors to open.

When the doors opened, we quickly ordered food and sat down. Niddy, Z-ooh, Robin, Ant-Nice, Wee, and I grabbed trays of food and sat at our usual table. We were the only PAs in the school today, and we got ominous looks from rival gangs in the lunchroom.

Black Mike and a full table of Seven Mile Gang bangers stared in delight at our present disadvantage. They were sitting only a few tables over, and talk of attacking the PAs was already circulating around the table.

"This would be a good time to rush them hoes while they numbers are small," said Romeo.

"Yeah, we could do that, but it would be stupid," Black Mike replied. "Security and the cops are waiting for us to do something like that. Look at how they are posted up by the walls and the doors." He pointed at the officers.

"Okay, you got a point, but when are we going to get them? It has to be today while they numbers are weak."

"We'll catch them slipping at our lockers after lunch is over, Romeo. Muscles and Niddy have a gym class by our lockers, and they walk through our hallway every day to get to that class. Well, today they either going to act like hoes and go the long way around to avoid us or they going to man up and continue they everyday journey through our halls. It really doesn't matter which way they go to class, because we going to make sure we have soldiers everywhere they turn before they make it to their class."

Black Mike's remarks left daunting images in his friends' heads. They knew he was right about our everyday pattern. And the way we had jumped Grimace and Ronald kept popping in their heads, creating a chaotic desire for revenge. Even the jumping of the PAs at the movie theater had left them no satisfaction.

While the Seven Mile Crew grumbled about their next move, we were eating our food without a care in the world. We knew the Sevens were watching us and were ready to fight at the drop of a dime. The object, though, was to play it off like we were slipping, so they would think they had the upper hand and attack us.

"Hey Niddy, you think them fools got enough balls to try and rush us?"

"I don't know, Z-ooh, just stay ready, dog; remember, them nigga's rushed Wee's boys at the Mercury."

"I doubt they fuck with us; hell, check out the security in here. They'll be fools to throw a fucking french fry in here," Ant-Nice said while finishing up his hamburger.

"Don't be a fool, Ant," I said boldly. "If they want us bad enough, they'll come for us in front of security."

"He's right," Robin told Ant-Nice, "but the biggest concern right now is how you, Niddy, and Muscles is going to make it to next class without getting bum-rushed by the Sevens if they don't attack us here."

"That's a good point, Robin," said Niddy. "We are the only PAs in the school right now, but Wee, Z-ooh, and you got to walk your way to class, and me, Muscles, and Ant got to get to ours."

"Listen," I said. "If you three walk us to the lockers, the Sevens would more than likely try and jump all of us, thinking we're trying to crew up in they hallway again. As much as I hate it, we just going to have to go to our gym classes the same way as usual, or don't go to the gym class at all."

When the bell rang, students stampeded out of the lunchroom like they were slaves being freed. Students who had their books with them went straight to class. My PA friends and I went to our lockers together, and then we split up and headed toward our classes as planned. Wee, Robin, and Z-ooh gave daps to us before they left, but they could not shake the feeling that they were making a mistake letting us go alone.

Niddy, Ant-Nice, and I walked into the neutral bathroom before we went to class, hoping to kill time until the Seven

Mile Gang left the hall. After ten minutes of chilling out in the bathroom, we left and began our dangerous journey.

All of us were quiet and focused when we walked through the hall that led to the gym class. We did not have a gun or brass knuckles, no weapons, nothing but heart and our clenched fists, fists we'd kept balled up since we left the bathroom. When we reached the end of the hall and turned down the next hallway, we saw Black Mike and a bunch of the Sevens.

The Seven Mile Gang was hanging ten deep in the hallway while most of the other students were already in class. Their laughter echoed through the building. All the laughing stopped when the three of us entered their hall. My two friends and I never looked at them. Instead, we stared straight ahead and prayed we would make it to the large gym doors without altercation. Avoiding eye contact with the Seven Mile Gang, however, was not enough as the whole gang stared us down like hawks eyeing their prey.

"PA down ain't shit, bitch!" Romeo yelled.

"You ain't shit, nigga!" Niddy retorted.

Niddy's reply caused all ten Seven Mile members to come off the lockers toward us, full of anger. Then, out of nowhere, Z-ooh ran up from the other direction and stood by our side. He quickly turned his Starter hat backward and got in a gorilla stance that made the Seven Mile Gang pause. The Seven Mile Gang then walked in front of us and stood their ground. They were face to face with their enemies for the first time this year, and Black Mike obviously enjoyed the advantage.

"Let's break these fools' backs, Black Mike; I've been waiting a long time for this, dog," Grimace said.

"Hold up, killers, I got something to say before we pop this shit off," Black Mike said, holding back his friends by extending both his arms. He stared Niddy down from head to toe and was surprised to see that the slim PA kid wasn't scared. Next he looked at me and the others and noticed that none of us were frightened either.

"You PA boys ain't tough. It's about time you motherfuckers recognize—" Black Mike said, and then he prepared to swing.

Suddenly, the gym teacher, Officer Jones, and Officer Brooks stormed out of the gymnasium doors. Every gang member in the hallway tried to run away at the sight of the officials. Although we all tried our best, Niddy, Black Mike, Romeo, Grimace, and I did not make it out of the hall. We were all grabbed and taken to the office.

Mr. Marksman, the counselor, stared at us in his office and shook his head in disgrace. When the officers had informed him last week that the majority of violence in the school was from gang violence, he had put out a specific order to catch gang bangers in the act and bring them to his office as soon as possible.

"Well, well, well. What do we have here? Wannabe gangsters, eh?" said the counselor. "You gangs had us fooled at first, but we've known that gangs have existed in the school for years. But this is the worst I have seen it in all the years I've worked here."

I frowned when the counselor looked at me; I knew after that statement, my days in Mumford were over. There was no use begging or kissing ass; whatever was going to happen was going to happen, regardless. Niddy and I were sitting away from Black Mike, Grimace, and Romeo. The gym teacher left the office and went back to class, but the two officers remained.

"Counselor, these are the leaders of two of the gangs in this school and probably behind some of the violence we can't solve," said Officer Jones.

"He's right; we were lucky to stop them before they killed each other by the gymnasium," Officer Brooks added.

"Well, they are going to be severely punished, that's for sure," Mr. Marksman said. "Is there anything you kids would like to say in your defense before I tell you my decision?"

"Yeah, I would like to say one thing," Niddy said, standing up. "All we were doing was going to class. They came and messed with us for nothing; we just stood our ground and defended ourselves. Ever since day one in school, our neighborhood had to get together and defend ourselves. The Seven Mile Gang and other gangs are Rich Boys who fool the everyday people. I live in the ghetto because I have to, unlike them Rich Boys, who do it because they want to be like us."

"What?" Black Mike said, rising out of his chair. "If you think we are some hoes just because we're not broke like you, then you are a bigger fool than I thought you were."

"Who the fuck you calling a fool and broke, bitch?"

"All right you two ... sit down, and I mean sit down now," Mr. Marksman said.

When Niddy and Black Mike sat down, Officer Jones took center stage in the office.

"Okay, I think I get it now," he said. "You guys over here are supposed to be the PA Crew, and you three over here are supposed to be the Seven Mile Crew. Man, I can't believe this shit. That same bullshit was going on when I was your age. The poor gang against the rich gang, the same shit. I will say one thing, though. You Rich Boys don't want any part of Puritan. Kids on that side of town grew up fighting over nickels and dimes."

Officer Jones's surprising comments left everyone in the office stunned. Even the counselor was shocked at what he said. Niddy and I tried to hide the smirks on our faces after the comments, but we were unsuccessful. It was the first time since joining the school that somebody gave our neighborhood that kind of props.

"All right, I've heard enough," Mr. Marksman said. "This is what I'm going to do. First, I'm suspending all you guys. Next, I'm going to make examples out of you, too, so that everyone else thinks twice about this gang nonsense." He stood up, and then he continued, "Officer Jones, I think there is only one thing these hard-headed kids will understand."

"I agree, and I am ready when you are, Mr. Marksman," the officer replied.

"Agree to what?" Romeo asked nervously.

"I'm about to send you idiots to a place you can fight all you want … you all are going to jail," Mr. Marksman said loudly.

"Going to jail?" Romeo said. "For what … when?"

"For gang banging; right now. Take them out of my sight, officers."

We were all so shocked at the decision that our mouths were still gaped wide open when the officers whipped out the handcuffs. None of us had expected to go to jail.

The bell rang just when we were being escorted out of the school. Kids quickly crowded the halls before we made it out of the building. All five of us looked straight ahead, even though everyone in the hall followed our every move till we were outside. In the past, some kids would enjoy the attention when they got in trouble. Today was different. All of us were ashamed and had sorrow painted on our faces. We all knew we were out of Mumford, and all of us knew we had some explaining to do to our parents.

The officers took us straight to the nearest precinct. We were booked, checked for weapons, allowed one phone call, and then tossed in the slammer. We were all put in separate cells that were separated by a narrow corridor. Grimace and I were in cells across from Niddy's, Romeo's, and Black Mike's cells. They were all impatiently waiting for their mothers to get them out, and it was starting to show.

"Man, this cell is driving me fucking nuts!" Grimace said. "I can't wait for my moms to get me the fuck out of here."

"Calm down, Grimace, before the turnkey hears you crying like a bitch," Black Mike said, bringing laughter from all the cells.

"He's right, there isn't any use bitching about this shit," Romeo said, after the laughter stopped. "They can't hold us that long, fuck no, we didn't do anything. We was about to fight, remember?"

"Yeah, I remember," Black Mike replied. "That's the only reason I didn't bother running from the bastards. I figure since we didn't do shit, why should I run? But look at the results."

While the two leaders from Seven Mile Road were talking, Niddy was digging in his sock.

"Hey Muscles, look what I got," he said, flashing a joint in front of the bars.

"How the hell you get that in here, man?" I asked. "When they were booking us, they checked us for everything."

"Except for this," Niddy replied, bringing laughter from all the cells again.

"Fire it up, Niddy," I said. "What are you waiting for?"

"Man, you must have lost your fucking mind," Niddy said. "If the turnkey smells that shit, they'll keep us forever."

"Your boy is right, Muscles, we trying to get out this motherfucker; if they smell that weed, they going to link it with all of us," said Romeo.

"I never thought I'd say this about somebody from Seven Mile," Niddy said. "But he's right."

I stared at Niddy, but after thinking about the situation for a minute, I realized they were right and I was wrong. The number one priority was to get the hell out of there, I concluded, not to do something to keep us there longer. After fifteen minutes, the turnkey opened the door, which made a loud clashing noise that echoed through the corridor. He went to Grimace's cell and told him he was being released. Grimace said good-bye to Romeo and Black Mike, and then he disappeared from everyone's sight when the doors slammed shut.

Ten minutes later, the turnkey returned and released Romeo; Black Mike was the lone Seven Mile member left in a cell. Hours went by, and we all expected to be released soon, especially after Grimace and Romeo's quick releases.

"We should be next," Niddy said.

"We must be," I said. "When, is the question."

"Both of you might as well get comfortable. We may be here all night," said Black Mike. "Romeo and Grimace are only fourteen years old, so they're still considered minors. That's probably why they were released so early and we're still here.

"We are minors too."

"Yeah, but we are older. Take it from somebody who been in and out of juvenile."

Niddy and I looked at Black Mike and wondered if he was lying, but realized the more he talked, the more everything he said made sense.

"I thought everyone under eighteen was considered a minor," Niddy said.

"They are, Niddy. I just have a habit of calling people fourteen and under minors. From my experience in jail, early releases were preserved for the youngest, so I been calling them minors ever since," said Black Mike.

"How old are you, Black Mike?" Niddy asked.

"Sixteen."

"That's the same age me and Muscles are."

"Yeah, I figured that," said Black Mike. "I knew off the top that you boys weren't minors."

We laughed at Black Mike's comment. The tension between the rival gangs was all but forgotten. We talked about peace and unity instead of beefing and fighting and promised to end the conflict in Mumford. We talked more and more; four hours passed by, totaling the number of hours spent in the cells to eight. Suddenly the loud noise from the corridor doors could be heard once more. This time Black Mike was released.

"You two brothers be cool, man. The first thing I'm going to do when I get back in the hood is holler at my boys on the peace tip."

"And we going to do the same when we get released, Black Mike; take care," Niddy said.

One hour later, Niddy was released, leaving me as the only one left in a cell. They brought me a small carton of milk and a dry baloney sandwich. I ate it like a starving animal, as hunger became my immediate concern. The weak meal just made me hungrier, but it eased the craving I had before I ate it.

When they finally released me from my cell, the turnkey took me to the booking area and gave me back my watch, keys, and school bag. I was given a court date and instructed to appear on that day. I took my belongings to the lobby, where my moms had been waiting impatiently.

14

Two weeks later, I found myself at the courthouse, ready to appear before the judge. The courthouse downtown was packed but very quiet when the judge entered the courtroom. The first people he called to the stand were Niddy, Black Mike, and me. Romeo and Grimace were not in the courtroom. I left my chair and stood directly in front of the judge. Ten days had gone by since we were released, and we all were anxious to get on with the process. We had been suspended indefinitely by the counselor, which left us with nothing to do during school hours.

The judge broke the courtroom silence. "Okay," he said, "after reading the complaint by Counselor Marksman, I have come to the conclusion that you three are gang bangers who don't deserve to be in school. You're troublemakers, mess starters, and above all you threaten everyone else's chance to learn. I'm kicking all three of you out of the whole Detroit public school system and sentencing you to one year of probation. And I want a monthly drug test and daily reports from your new school. If your grades are less than a 'C' or you flunk a drug test or refuse to go to school, you will get a one-year sentence in the slammer; understand?"

All three of us nodded our heads in agreement. "Good, I will allow you to go back to Mumford one day next week to

183

take your finals; that will be your last day. Now, if you want to act like a bunch of badasses when you go to Mumford that day, I'll give you two years' probation and a longer alternative sentence."

The judge slammed his gavel and said our cases were dismissed. Niddy and I left the courtroom with our heads down, while Black Mike's face looked shocked. None of us could believe we had been given such a harsh sentence. The probation and drug test every month were no big deal. But not being allowed back in Mumford after the finals was unbearable. The dreams Niddy and I had of graduating from Mumford had just gone out the window.

One week later, all of us were back in school to take our finals in our main classes. The truant officers escorted us to our classes. When Niddy and I were led to our English literature class, I sat down with pure confidence. I knew I would pass the test. I had studied the whole week and was clean from the pot smoking. Niddy, on the other hand, sat down with uncertainty. English wasn't one of his better classes, so he planned to pass the test by sitting next to me and cheating. I didn't mind, especially knowing Niddy would have done the same for me.

We finished the test and received our grades fifteen minutes later. We both passed with a "B." Our test results were good in our other classes too.

When Niddy and I left the school, we saw Black Mike and Romeo posted up in the parking lot. As we approached them, twenty unknown Seven Mile members appeared at their side and stopped right in front of us.

Black Mike stepped up to Niddy and me and said, "The beef is over, right? It been quiet all week. I like to keep it like that, quiet."

"We have no problem with being quiet; as long as you brothers stay quiet, we will be quiet," I said.

"Well, I think we are proving that by not attacking you guys with our advantages," said Romeo.

"What advantages? Turn around and check that out," Niddy said, pointing outside the parking lot.

Black Mike and his friends turned around and couldn't believe what they saw. There were six cars loaded with PAs waiting outside the parking lot like watchdogs.

Epilogue

his story happened twenty-seven years ago. My turbulent years as a teenager in Mumford led to many setbacks for me, as the streets became a big part of my life. Although I eventually graduated, I never fulfilled my late father's dream of finishing college and becoming a success like he was. I wasted ten years of my life in the street before I realized the life of gang banging, selling crack, and smoking pot was a dead end. After being spared by the great lord many times in the street, I knew I was meant to do something more in life. I left Detroit, moved to Louisiana when I was twenty-seven years old, and got a nine-to-five job at a hospital.

I would be a liar if I said my problems were over once I arrived in my new home. I got in fights and shoot-outs, and I got caught up in different wars with different gangs in a different city. However, living in a smaller city taught me humility and responsibility, which had not been possible in Detroit. The gang mentality I carried with me off the Greyhound bus eventually faded from my mind, and I proceeded to live a square life. With the exception of my PA homeys Otis, Buddy, Little Robby, Perpin-Norm, and OG-Greg (rest in peace), my PA friends are all alive and well. Niddy, who received his diploma the same day I received mine, now works every day instead of hustling in the street like he used to do. My friends and I get together every year and talk about old times and about how much our lives have changed.

Unfortunately, all the gangs that were mentioned in this story still exist to this very day. In fact, years later the PA Gang's numbers grew so much in Mumford that all three of the mile gangs formed together against them and started calling themselves the 678 Boys.

In my opinion, I think there wouldn't be any gangs if it wasn't for the ghettos, and as long as there are ghettos, there will always be gangs. Instead of society focusing on why the school systems are what they are, we should be seizing the opportunity to change the structure of the ghetto. When upper middle class neighborhoods start producing gangs, it means the problem has spread.